Lewis and Clark in the Twenty-First Century is an excellent resource tool for teaching because it is a modern day perspective set in the 1800s; it is more accessible to our young learners…

—David Haugen
assistant professor
Ohio University

Scholl has meticulously catalogued a journey that is like no other. *Lewis and Clark in the Twenty-First Century* gives a new perspective and reverence for the sacrifices of our great explorers and settlers.

—Rebekah Slotnick
educator

Lewis and Clark in the Twenty-First Century is a revelation. It is a detailed and inspiring account of two epic journeys. The reader is granted an unparalleled view of the patchwork of people and places that make up this great nation.

—Julie Germano
a Lewis and Clark junkie

To: Tom Vorhees

I am proud to inscribe this copy of my book about our 200th anniversary reenactment of the Lewis and Clark Expedition to you, a former United States naval pilot and a true American patriot. I know you share with me the wonders and amazement I have always had for the bravery and daring of that small band of early patriots who made the original Corps of Discovery and so amazed the world with their exploits. Your sister in Florida

LEWIS AND CLARK

IN THE TWENTY-FIRST CENTURY

has told me of your love of the Lewis and Clark story and I hope that our recent reenactment of their journey is worthy of the place in history that expedition has earned.

Ed Scholl
as Pvt HUGH HALL
a fellow Pennsylvanian
"We Proceeded On"

LEWIS *&* CLARK
IN THE TWENTY-FIRST CENTURY

Colonel Ed Scholl, USAR, Retired

TATE PUBLISHING & *Enterprises*

Published by Tate Publishing & Enterprises, LLC
127 E. Trade Center Terrace | Mustang, Oklahoma 73064 USA
1.888.361.9473 | www.tatepublishing.com

Tate Publishing is committed to excellence in the publishing industry. The company reflects the philosophy established by the founders, based on Psalm 68:11,
"The Lord gave the word and great was the company of those who published it."

Published in the United States of America
ISBN: 978-1-61663-055-3
1. History: United States: General
2. Travel: Special Interest: General
10.06.03

Table of Contents

Foreword

It was not until I arrived in Elizabeth, Pennsylvania, from New York City, that I fully realized my father was completely serious and totally immersed in the Lewis and Clark reenactment. It was breathtaking to see the very first launch; for these men and women it was a journey that would keep them in and out of each other's lives over the next three years. I met my father while on his journey two more times over the next three years as I moved from New York to Los Angeles to Ohio. Each time I arrived at camp, I was immediately possessed by the spirit of these men and women, who respectfully and authentically carried out their mission to follow these covered and paved-over footsteps.

My father has always been a writer, so it was not a surprise to learn that he was journaling about his time on this expedition. But it did surprise me that he planned to write a book about his experiences and share these experiences with the world. By the end of this journey my father had turned seventy-six years old, one of the "wisest" reenactment members among the ranks.

It has been an honor and inspiration to help edit and shape this book with my father. Thank you, Dad, for following your heart.

—Kate Scholl

Introduction

The United States obtained the Louisiana Purchase in March 1804, from France, and this purchase doubled the size of the United States. The Louisiana Purchase was defined as all the land which made up the Mississippi Watershed west of the Mississippi River. Basically it was all of the land from which the water flowed into the Mississippi River. President Jefferson needed as much information about this area as possible. He envisioned a military expedition exploring this area in order to find a water way to the Pacific Ocean for the purpose of commerce. President Jefferson's thirst for knowledge included the plants, animals, minerals, soil, and the cultures of people living in the area.

There was also an area beyond the Louisiana Purchase that had to be explored. President Jefferson tasked Captain Meriwether Lewis with leading an expedition to gather as much information as possible about the two areas, keeping a journal during his travels across the unknown expanse of the territory west of the United States. Captain Lewis then tasked Captain Clark to keep a journal.

This book is being written to commemorate and chronicle the journey of the Discovery Expedition of Saint Charles, Missouri, as its members reenacted the original Lewis and Clark Expedition. This book also documents the efforts of my fellow crewmembers and the assistance that all of the people across this wonderful country of ours gave us. It contains information for the "Clarkies," who are familiar with the efforts of the original expedition and information for persons who have a little knowledge or no knowledge of the 1803–1806 expedition.

One of the questions I am invariably asked is how I got involved with this reenactment. I joined the Discovery Expedition of Saint Charles, Missouri, in 2001 after taking an Elderhostel program. The Elderhostel organization presents programs for continuing education for senior citizens. They offer 6,000 programs in the United States and 2,000 programs overseas. In September 2001, I took a Lewis and Clark Elderhostel program. There were forty-two of us on the bus, which took eighteen days to travel from Saint Charles, Missouri, to Fort Clatsop, Oregon. We saw all of the highlights experienced by the men on the original expedition. When I had seen what these men had seen and done, I had to get involved. Upon my return home, I surfed the Internet and found that this organization, The Discovery Expedition of Saint Charles, Missouri, was planning a reenactment of the original expedition. I sent them an e-mail that I was interested, and I received an e-mail saying, "Welcome Aboard." The rest is history.

I hope you enjoy our efforts in duplicating the trail emblazoned by the supermen of the 1803–1806 expedition.

Preparation for the Journey

The Plan

In 1803, a sergeant in the United States Army had to be able to write in order to be a sergeant. Consequently, the sergeants on the expedition were, in addition to Lewis and Clark, tasked to keep journals. These journals were so detailed that they gave us minute information about the trials and tribulations of the men and an intimate look at what the men saw. The journals of the men of the original expedition set the timeline and established the camping sites for us.

During the expedition there were three sergeants keeping journals. Sergeants John Ordway, Patrick Gass, and Charles Floyd all have had their journals published. Private Joseph Whitehouse also kept a journal, and it was subsequently published. I believe that Sergeant Nathaniel Pryor also kept a journal because he was a sergeant, but his journal has never surfaced for publication. Private Robert Frazer kept a journal, but this journal has never been found.

Most of our expedition members were not on the river for the entire trip. Since we were all volunteers, we put as much time on the river as we could. In the beginning, we were not sure how we could handle sleeping on boats and in tents night after night. Therefore, the guidance was to go on the river for two weeks, go home for two weeks to recharge our batteries, and then return to the river for another two weeks.

The original expedition was on the river for sixteen weeks in 1803. Following the recommendation, I spent eight weeks on the river the first year. A second reason for this was to give other men a chance to participate, because if I spent sixteen weeks on the river, this would preclude other men from enjoying this once-in-a-life-time adventure.

There were a handful of men, known as cadre, who did spend additional time on the river for continuity's sake. We had over 200 men and women enlisted as crewmembers. Not all 200 could participate at the same time. An average number of twenty-five to thirty men on the river at one time would be sufficient. The smallest number of men on the river at one time was twelve, and the largest was eighty-three. We had difficulty sailing boats and performing ground crew assignments with only twelve people.

When we crossed the Mississippi River and started up the Missouri River in May of 2004, we lost a lot of men from Pennsylvania, Ohio, Indiana, and Illinois. Consequently, the word went out to schedule as much time on the river as we wished. As a result, I spent nine weeks on the river in 2004.

In 1805, the original expedition was on the river for eight months, and I spent six months on the river during 2005. I live in the Philadelphia, Pennsylvania area, and it is a five-hour drive from Philadelphia to Pittsburgh, Pennsylvania. When our expedition was on the Ohio River, this driving time was acceptable. But as the expedition went farther and farther west, the driving time increased. Saint Louis is a one-night drive. Fort Mandan, North Dakota, is a two-night drive. Great Falls, Montana is a three-night drive, and Fort Clatsop, Oregon is a four-night drive. Traveling these distances for two weeks on the river is not worth the effort or cost. Consequently, the farther west the expedition went, the more time I spent on the river.

In 2006, the expedition spent six months on the river, and I spent the entire six months on the river. As a result, I was with the expedition for 77 percent of the entire three-year trip. Many of our younger men have jobs, families, mortgages, and car payments. Consequently, they are limited to the time they can be on the river. Some of our men spent their two-week annual vacation on the river. We have had men join us for a weekend when we were close to their homes. Then there are some of us who are retired and can spend as much time on the river as we wish because every day is a vacation day. The average age of the men on the original expedition was twenty-seven. Our average age was fifty-seven. I am a retired army colonel, and this military expedition was right down my alley.

Supplies

Just as Meriwether Lewis did 200 years ago, we needed training, uniforms, accouterments, and other sundry items.

Starting with training, our organization required all crewmembers to undergo on the river training. The training consisted of complete familiarization with the boat and its compartments. This training was normally given at dockside. Then we would be taken out onto the river and were shown how to handle the boat and go through a man overboard drill. This drill included the proper use of the throw rope and other life-saving equipment and procedures. During our entire trip, we were very safety conscious, and each member of the crew would remind another member if it seemed that a safety procedure was being violated. We were told over and over not to put your back to the river because the river is unforgiving.

Consequently, we were blessed by having only minor injuries during our three-year journey. As a point of interest, the original expedition did not have things like life-saving throw ropes or life vests. We will talk more about other things we were required to have that were not required 200 years ago. Times have changed. Our expedition had a foot in two different centuries. We try to maintain uniforms and firearms of the nineteenth century, but realize that we do live in the twenty-first century with all of its comforts and amenities, which includes Band-Aids and cell phones.

In order to be a captain of one of the boats, our organization highly suggested that the individual take a United States Coast Guard Water Safety and Navigation Course. Most, if not all, of our captains did take these courses. Our travels took us onto navigable waters such as the Ohio River, the Mississippi River, the Missouri River, and the Columbia River. We were traveling with and next to ocean going vessels. We also had river charts to read and had to be familiar with channel markings, buoy colors, river mile markings, no wake areas, know danger areas, restricted areas, locks at many of the dams and dozens of other water hazards, and boater's responsibilities. The original expedition did not have some of the impediments we faced in the twenty-first century. They had free-flowing unimpeded water, except for rapids and falls, during their entire journey.

Another form of training was physical training taken at the responsibility of each individual. It is very strenuous to handle the boats, whether it be the keelboat, pirogues, or dugout canoes. Pulling up anchors, throwing ropes, muscling boats into position, carrying supplies, pitching and taking tents down almost daily, loading and unloading trailers daily, chopping firewood, and numerous other activities required muscle and physical stamina on a daily basis. We also had marching drills, firearms inspections, guard duty, kitchen police, boat watch, and many other duties necessary for a successful expedition. As you can see, we did almost everything the members of the original did. They were supermen, and I guess that makes us supermen.

Our uniforms and accouterments were of the 1804 period. Quite often, visitors to our camps and schoolchildren asked, "Where did you get your uniforms and muskets?" For posterity purposes, I will list how I assembled my necessary equipment. Captain Lewis used various sources for assembling the camp equipment and provisions, navigation instruments, Indian presents, medicines, and military supplies and material that would be necessary to complete the Corps of Discovery's journey. He purchased many items in Philadelphia. He also requisitioned military supplies from the Schuylkill Arsenal in Philadelphia and Harper's Ferry Arsenal in Virginia. The members of our crew also used many sources to find the items needed for our journey. Just like the original men of the corps, we wore cloth clothing at the beginning of our adventure. Their clothing started wearing out about halfway through the expedition. Since there were no Walmarts in 1805, the original members of the expedition turned to leather for clothing. We did the same thing.

Here is a list of necessary items, where they were obtained, and the cost. Captain Lewis had a similar list of items and procurement sources.

Item(s)	Source	Cost
Blue Coat	Historic Costume Designs, St. Louis, MO	$285.00
Vest	Historic Costume Designs, St. Louis, MO	55.00
Two Shirts	Historic Costume Designs, St. Louis, MO	64.00
Pants	Historic Costume Designs, St. Louis, MO	59.00
Fatigue Hat	Historic Costume Designs, St. Louis, MO	34.00
Hat w/Bear Fur	Fellow member	100.00

Gaiters	J. Higgins Ltd., Lenexa, KS	45.00
Musket, Tomahawk, Powder Horn	Collector's Armoury Ltd., Lorton, VA	191.80
Belt, Hunting Frock, Hat, Cup, Canteen, Haversack	Jas Townsend and Son Inc., Pierceton, IN	182.60
Scabbard, Cartridge, Box, Hunting Bag, Sling, Tomahawk, Frog	Sutler of Mount Misery, Valley Forge, PA	168.38
Pockets in hunting Frock	Local tailor	12.00
Period Glasses	Jas Townsend and son Inc, Pierceton, IN	31.00
Lenses for glasses	Dr Morris, Hatboro, PA	60.00
Wood dinner bowl	Goodwill, Lansdale, PA	3.99
DESC membership	Discovery Expedition of Saint Charles, MO	35.00
Lewis Coat	Historic Costume Designs, St. Louis, MO	265.00
Duffle Bag	Willow Grove NAS, Willow Grove, PA	35.00
Poncho	Fort Dix, NJ	35.00
Barracks Bag, Pillow	Bed, Bath and Beyond, Philadelphia, PA	14.93
Mosquito Repeller	Boater's World, Philadelphia, PA	10.00
Ground Cloth, Sleeping Pad	Fort Dix, NJ	53.35
Pants, Neck Stock, Buttons, Tomahawk,	Jas Townsend and Son Inc., Pierceton, IN	86.00
Poncho	Crazy Crow, Pottsboro, TX	25.95

Cot	REI, Seattle, WA	73.14
Suspenders, Buttons, Spoon, Bungee	Dixon Muzzleloading, Kempton, PA	41.80
Neck Stock, Gaiters and alterations	Sutler of Mount Misery, Valley Forge, PA	91.95
Emergency Evacuation	Diver's Alert Network, Durham, NC	29.00
Knife, Sheath	Dixon Muzzleloading, Kempton, PA	34.98
Duffle Bag	Crazy Crow, Pottsboro, TX	15.95
Oilskin Raincoat	Fellow member	80.00
Oilskin Hood	Panther Primitives, Normantown, WV	37.57
Shoes	Payless Shoes, Kansas City, MO	21.46
Period Glasses	Jas Townsend and Son Inc, Pierceton, IN	32.00
Lenses for glasses	Dr Morris, Hatboro, PA	68.00
Travel Clock	Radio Shack, Philadelphia, PA	15.89
Thermarest Pad	REI, Seattle, WA	21.15
Longjohns	Sears, Philadelphia, PA	12.98
DESC membership	Discovery Expedition of Saint Charles, MO	50.00
Emergency Evacuation (Second Year)	Diver's Alert Network, Durham, NC	29.00
Face Guard	Ski Shop, Philadelphia, PA	15.99

Under Armor	Modell's, Philadelphia, PA	39.99
Two Blankets	Discovery Expedition of Saint Charles, MO	222.00
Moccasins	Al Puknat, St. Louis, MO	60.00
Moccasins Insole	Walgreen's, Dillon, MT	19.99
Capote	Historic Costume Designs, St. Louis, MO	250.00
Sleeping Mat	Sports Authority, Philadelphia, PA	52.98
Life Jacket	Cabela's, Hamburg, PA	31.75
Leather	Fellow member	66.00
Leather Shirt	Fellow member	225.00
Lead Cannister	Richard Anderson, Astoria, OR	75.00
DESC membership	Discovery Expedition of Saint Charles, MO	50.00
Shirt	Panther Primitives, Normantown, WV	36.75
Leather Pants, Moccasins	River Spirit, Klicitat, WA	245.00
Total		**$3,897.32**

This is more than Captain Lewis was authorized by Congress in 1803 for the entire expedition, which was $2,500. Captain Lewis actually spent approximately $36,000 during his journey. This $36,000 was in 1803 dollars. You can do the math for its equivalency in today's dollars.

There are additional costs for maintaining our equipment such as dry-cleaning for wool articles, thread and needles for repairs, oils and lubricants for weapons and leather, leather punches and hammers, and on and on.

Captain Lewis carried three sizes of Jefferson Peace Medals on the Lewis and Clark Expedition. He had three large medals, thirteen medium size medals, and fifteen or sixteen small medals. The Discovery Expedition of Saint Charles designed a gift medal depicting the keelboat on the front and the Jefferson Peace and Friendship Medal on the back. These medals were gold and silver. The medals were given to people who assisted the corps during its journey. It would not surprise me if seven or eight hundred medals were presented to worthy recipients.

Another area of expertise that required multiple hours of training and/or research was becoming familiar with the Lewis and Clark story. Reading books, publications, and articles on all facets of the trip was imperative in order to properly interact with visitors and schoolchildren.

Each member of our crew was required to portray a member of the original expedition. I chose Private Hugh Hall. I am from Philadelphia, Pennsylvania and Private Hall was from Carlisle, Pennsylvania. Therefore, I was portraying a fellow Pennsylvanian, and that was cool. More about Private Hall in a later chapter.

The Discovery Expedition of Saint Charles, Missouri had a primary mission of telling the story of the Lewis and Clark Expedition to as many people as possible, as we traveled the trail. As individuals, we were tasked with the same mission. In order to do this properly, we must be fully versed in as many areas of the Lewis and Clark journey as possible. Consequently, reading books, publications, articles, and attending conferences and seminars were all necessary to accrue the information needed for our reenactment.

It was totally fun to sit around a fire at night and speak about little-known facts of the original expedition. With the fire and stars as our candles, we would exchange information which we could use the next day in our presentations to the public. These are the times that I miss so very much. I can see how the men of the original expedition bonded. Of course, their bonding was one of necessity. Our bonding was founded on a mutual respect for each other. Just like the original men, we know each others' strengths and weaknesses. And just like the men of the original expedition, our men are from all walks of life with different interests, backgrounds, and skills. Consequently, if a question was asked by a visitor, someone in our camp had the answer. It is amazing how our men responded in a time of need and pulled together.

Once our preparation was complete, we proceeded on.

The Rivers

The interstate highways of the early 1800s were the rivers. Consequently, the Native Americans and the settlers that traveled west followed rivers when possible.

President Jefferson requested Captain Meriwether Lewis to find a waterway across the continent for the benefit of commerce to the west. Jefferson envisioned an easy waterway connecting to the Columbia River and then to the Pacific Ocean.

As we followed the tracks of the original Corps of Discovery, we traveled on the Monongahela River (22 miles), the Ohio River (973 miles), the Mississippi River (192 miles), the Missouri River (2540 miles), the Clearwater River (70 miles), the Snake River (140 miles), and the Columbia River (325 miles) on our journey to the Pacific Ocean. On our return trip, we also traveled on the Yellowstone River.

The rivers have changed in the past 200 years. The only free-flowing river we traveled on was the Clearwater River. The good folks in Montana will say that the Yellowstone River is not dammed. This is true. There are no large concrete dams such as Boulder Dam or the Grand Coulee Dam, but the Yellowstone has diversion dams which impeded our dugout canoes. Even though these dams were only a foot or two high, we could not get our canoes safely over them. We had to portage around the dams.

The Monongahela River had one dam on it between Elizabeth, Pennsylvania, and Pittsburgh, Pennsylvania. This dam did have a lock, which meant that we did not have to portage around the dam.

There are twenty dams on the Ohio River between Pittsburgh and the confluence at the Mississippi River. All of these dams have locks. The greatest drop is approximately sixty-five feet at the falls of the Ohio near Louisville, Kentucky, and Clarksville, Indiana. The smallest drop is approximately nine feet. Consequently, the Ohio River is a river of lakes. The first hundred miles or so from Pittsburgh was like going through an alley. The banks of the river are highly industrialized with concrete retaining walls, abutments, piers, warehouses, and other industrial structures. There are very few banks with trees coming down to the water's edge. But once we left this industrialized portion of the Ohio, the trees met the water and the landscape changed radically. It was a pleasure to put the boats onto a river's bank for a night's camping.

I must compliment the Corps of Engineers and their lockmasters because they were very accommodating. We went through all of their locks across the entire country without a problem. There were many times when our boats were the only boats in the lock. We did not have to wait for other river traffic in order to proceed on. As a point of interest, we had to don life jackets to traverse their locks. The men on the original expedition did not have life jackets, but then they did not have locks to travel through either. As another point of interest, when we were on the Snake River and the Columbia River, we were in dugout canoes. Since these canoes were not motorized, we could not sit in them while traversing the locks. But we were still required to wear our life jackets. We had to tie up to a motorized boat, leave the dugouts, and board the motorized boat while going through the locks. The Washington National Guard helped us here because they had four motorized Zodiacs that accompanied us all the way through Washington on our way to the Pacific as a safety factor.

Speaking of safety factors, several organizations and states provided assistance and help on the rivers. The Corps of Engineers had a towboat with a barge travel with us down the Ohio River. The state of Missouri, Conservation Department furnished a boat and men to provide a safety net for us. The North Dakota National Guard furnished two-bridge building boats to assists us, going through low water areas of the Missouri River while in their state. The Montana National Guard helped us with trucks moving our boats and storage when necessary. A sheriff's department in Idaho assigned a patrol boat to us as a safety net. Even the United States Coast Guard Auxiliary furnished a boat to assist us, if needed, while we were on the Columbia River on our way to Fort Clatsop. On our return trip from the Pacific, a Washington state sheriff's department assigned a rescue boat to us for aid, if needed. I apologize to any organization or individual who had helped us and I have not recognized them.

It may sound like we were not alone on the rivers, and we were not. Just remember that the Indians helped the original Corps of Discovery in their times of need. Indians showed the members of the Corps how to burn out the center of the dugout logs instead of using metal implements because the Indians did not have metal implements. The Indians also traded for canoes, boats, and horses, as needed. They showed the Corps trails and advised them of which way to travel. The Corps was saved several times by the friendliness of the Native Americans. We were no different in the treatment and help we received from the locals as we crossed this grand and beautiful country of ours.

Another point of interest on our journey was July 4, 2004. We were in Atchison, Kansas, to celebrate the Fourth, just like the original expedition. This is less than three years after 9/11. Our country was very active in protecting its national heritage symbols. Our expedition was considered a national symbol and considered a terrorist target. As we left Atchison, four sea doos followed us for two days just shepherding us for safety's sake.

In our travels up the Mississippi River, we did not encounter any dams below the confluence of the Missouri River. There is a dam a short distance above this confluence at Alton, Illinois. Our boats were moored in the Alton Marina and consequently had to pass through Lock 26 on the Mississippi River on several occasions.

As we started our journey up the Missouri River on May 14, 2004, we encountered the spring runoff. The river was full of logs, tree limbs, empty barrels, refrigerators, plastic bottles, and anything thing else that would float. We needed a man on the front of each boat to direct the helms man in order not to ram major debris floating in the water. I am sure that the original Corps of Discovery encountered a spring runoff, but not of the magnitude we encountered. Things have changed in 200 years.

During our first thirty days on the Missouri River, I believe it rained twenty-five of those days. It was very uncomfortable wearing wet clothes day after day. The journals also are full of comments about the wet rainy weather, so I guess some things may not have changed in 200 years.

There are six dams on the Missouri River administered by the Army Corps of Engineers. They are the Gavin's Point Dam, the Fort Randall Dam, the Big Bend Dam, the Oahe Dam, the Garrison Dam, and the Fort Peck Dam. None of these dams have locks. Therefore, it was necessary to portage around each one on the dams.

We were informed that North Dakota and Montana have been in a seven-year drought. Once we pulled our boats out of the water for a portage, we could normally put them back in the water just above the dam. But when you travel twenty miles upstream, some of the boat ramps no longer meet the water. Consequently, there were times we had to bypass a river float. This problem required a constant advance scouting of the upstream portions of our trip. Once again, things have changed because the original expedition did not experience such difficulties.

The drought also left us with low water. It was not unusual to ground a boat on an unseen sandbar. It was also very difficult to find a deep enough channel through the myriad of channels that presented themselves to us. At times, a sounding pole was used almost constantly on the bow of the boats. These problems existed until the large boats were no longer used going upstream because the water was too shallow. The keelboat was returned to Saint Louis upon our departure from Fort Mandan in the spring of 2005. The pirogues were abandoned a short distance downstream from the Great Falls. When all three boats were traveling together, the two pirogues would normally precede the keelboat because they needed less water for drafting.

Once we ran out of water near Dillon, Montana, we crossed the Bitterroot Mountains on the Lolo Trail on horseback. We arrived at canoe camp near Orofino, Idaho and spent two weeks here making two dugout canoes. Three dugouts had already been made by the Hog Heaven Muzzleloaders. We entered the Clearwater River with our dugouts. The Clearwater River is the only undammed river we traversed on our travels across the country. There were white water rapids on the Clearwater. Shortly after entering the Clearwater River, one of our dugouts capsized in the white water. All hands survived.

Upon completing our run of approximately seventy miles down the Clearwater River, we entered the Snake River at Lewiston, Idaho. We traveled 140 miles down the Snake River to its confluence with the Columbia River. It was extremely pleasant to travel downstream with the current instead of fighting an upstream current, as we had done on the other side of the Rocky Mountains.

Our travels on the Snake River took us through four locks at four dams. Each lock had a one hundred-foot drop. This is equivalent to a ten-story building. I was really impressed with the magnitude of these dams and their locks. Just like the Missouri River and the Clearwater River, the Snake River winds through beautiful vistas of our country in its travels to join the Columbia River. The trees seem greener and the sky seems bluer along these ribbons of water. I can appreciate the original corps' admiration for the views they had experienced.

Upon reaching the confluence of the Snake River with the Columbia River, we were 325 miles from the Pacific Ocean. Between this point and the Pacific Ocean there were four more dams with locks. Each lock was, again, a one hundred-foot drop. Even though we had traversed four similar dams on the Snake River, I was still impressed with the magnitude of each of these locks. Their overwhelming size compared to our insignificantly small dugout canoes was awesome.

The Columbia River travels through a semi-arid eastern Washington and Oregon until it arrives at The Dalles. Then the weather changes radically to rain almost day after day. It seems that the Cascade Mountains are a natural barrier to weather patterns west of the mountains because we were wet more than we were dry on this portion of our travels to the Pacific Ocean.

The Columbia River gorge is one of the most beautiful gorges in the world, with its majestic walls, waterfalls, treeless vistas, and then trees all through the Cascade Mountains. It is something to see. It was a phenomenal journey for us as well as the original corps.

Then, "Ocian in view! O! the joy." There we were at Station Camp, the estuary of the Columbia River, and the Pacific Ocean. It was quite exhilarating to have completed this journey just like the men did 200 years ago.

The Boats

The reenactment of the 200-year commemoration of the Lewis and Clark Expedition was the dream of our mentor, Glen Bishop, a master boatwright and resident of Saint Charles, Missouri. Some thirteen years before the 2003–2006 expedition, Bishop built a model of the keelboat. It was a one-inch- to one-foot-scale replica. The dimensions can be found in the journals. Upon completion of his model keelboat, Bishop then decided to build an exact replica of the original keelboat. He toiled for several years, and with the help of several friends, he completed the boat. His keelboat was fifty-five feet long and eight feet wide. It weighed nine tons and could carry about nine tons of cargo. The boat was stored in a warehouse that caught fire in 1996, and the boat was destroyed. This did not deter Bishop. He immediately proceeded to build another better keelboat. This boat was finished in 1999 and made its maiden voyage the same year. It was due to Bishop's persistence and undaunted spirit that gave birth to the Discovery Expedition of Saint Charles, Missouri and the 2003–2006 Reenactment. Unfortunately, Glen Bishop passed away in October of 2001.

Following completion of the keelboat, Bishop then proceeded to build replicas of the thirty-nine-foot white pirogue and the forty-one-foot red pirogue. Once again, he used the information found in the journals to construct these boats.

There is some question as to where the original keelboat was built. Some historians believe that it was built in Elizabeth, Pennsylvania, and others believe that it was built in Pittsburgh, Pennsylvania. Either way, it was loaded in Pittsburgh, Pennsylvania and started down the Ohio River on August 31, 1803.

Upon arrival at Wheeling, Virginia (West Virginia did not become a state until 1863), Captain Lewis had additional supplies waiting for him on the dock. Consequently, he needed an additional boat. He purchased the red pirogue in Wheeling, loaded his supplies, and continued on down the Ohio River.

Upon arrival at Fort Kaskaskia, Illinois Territory, he found that he needed another boat because his crew was too large for the two boats he had been using. He requisitioned the white pirogue from the United States Army stationed at Fort Kaskaskia. This now gave him the three boats he needed for his crew to travel up the Missouri River to the Mandans.

All three of these boats could be moved in four different ways. The boats could be rowed, sailed, poled, or cordelled (pulled with a rope). All four methods were used by the original crews.

Since we were traveling on navigable waters, the United States Coast Guard required that boats the size of ours be motor driven so that they could get out of the way of towboats and other commercial vessels. These regulations applied to the Ohio River, the Mississippi River, the Lower Missouri River, the Snake River, and the Columbia River. Consequently, our keelboat was equipped with a 150-horsepower Mercury marine engine, and both pirogues had a seventy-horsepower outboard motor for propulsion. All modern equipment was stowed so as not to detract from period correctness. Once we had an engine or motor on board the craft, the Coast Guard then required us to have a fire extinguisher on board. As stated earlier, we were also required to have a life jacket on board for each crewmember. As we approached a lock for one of the dams, we had to radio ahead to the lockmaster our location and intent to use the lock. This required that we have radios on board the boats. We had no plans on running at night, so we did not need running lights. Things have changed in 200 years.

During our travels up the Missouri River, we had the option of sleeping either on the boats or in tents. The keelboat could comfortably accommodate ten men. Each of the pirogues could accommodate six men. I had a preference to sleep in a tent because of the river moisture early in the morning. If you have been around boats, you know that it is not unusual to have a boat covered with dew when at anchor. This same problem can be found when camping out, but it is not as prevalent as when you are at dockside. The positive side of sleeping on a boat is that you do not have to pitch a tent every night.

Our boats were tented for sleeping. That is, a line was tied from bow to stern and canvas was thrown over the line to cover the deck and locker areas. This helped prevent moisture from forming on your sleeping gear, and it also kept the rain off you.

We had rain on twenty-five of thirty days as we started our travels up the Missouri River in 2004. It was a very disheartening experience, but the journals are full of comments about rain and bad weather 200 years ago. Therefore, we were only experiencing the trials and tribulations the men on the original trip experienced. Since this was a once-in-a-lifetime opportunity to be part of living history, we persevered and finally had hot weather to complain about a short time later. Our shoes finally dried out somewhere in South Dakota.

The keelboat was the jewel of our expedition, and the pirogues were accompanying gems. Wherever we docked or pulled up onto the bank, we were greeted by warm and wonderful people. Our admirers were full of envy and questions. It made us proud to be able to walk in the footsteps of those wonderful men who went before us. They did not know what to expect on their epic journey—neither did we. But just like them, we accepted the daily adventures as they unfolded.

We were unable to live off the land like they did 200 years ago, but the people along the way made sure that we did not starve. I ate more donated buffalo and elk in six months than I had eaten in my entire life.

All three boats arrived at Fort Mandan on November 2, 2004, just like the original expedition. Rather than stay in North Dakota for the winter, we disbanded and went our separate ways until April of 2005.

On April 7, 1805, the keelboat was sent back to Saint Louis with about ten men aboard. Corporal Warfington was in command, and the crew included Privates Newman and Reed, who had been court-martialed and prevented from continuing the journey. The engages (hired boatmen) were also sent back at this time. The two pirogues and six dugout canoes made by the men of the expedition continued up the Missouri River.

It was during their stay in the Mandan Village area that the men were introduced to bullboats. These boats were not used at this time, but they became very useful during their travels on the Yellowstone River. More about bullboats will be discussed in later chapters.

Our modern-day journey proceeded up the Missouri River from Fort Mandan with the two pirogues and two dugout canoes made by the Missouri Conservation Department. These canoes were on loan to us for the remainder of our trip. We wish to acknowledge them and thank them for their generosity.

In 1805, near the confluence of the Maris River, the red pirogue was left on the riverbank. Near the lower portage camp, the white pirogue was cached. The men then proceeded to portage the six dugouts around the Great Falls.

We were lucky because all of our boats had modern-day trailers for portaging. Our two pirogues were trailered and returned to Saint Charles. We proceeded on with two dugouts till we ran out of water at Camp Fortunate (Clark Reservoir near Dillon, Montana).

During our travels on this leg of the journey, we ran into low water problems. The Dakotas and Montana were in a seven-year drought period. As mentioned before, there are six large dams on the upper Missouri River. We had no problems putting our boats into the water above the dams, but if you went twenty miles up the river, the boat ramps no longer reached the water. Therefore, we could not get our boats onto their trailers for portaging. Consequently, there were some parts of the journey that we could not paddle. These setbacks were not common but equal to some of the setbacks the original expedition experienced.

After crossing the Bitterroot Mountains on horseback, we arrived at Canoe Camp, which is just west of Orofino, Idaho.

Here, we built two dugout canoes with tools of the period. We were in Canoe Camp for two weeks, as per the original expedition, and sweated just like they did during our efforts. The original crew made five dugouts during that time period with thirty-two men. We had about half that number in our crew, so we only made two dugouts. We were lucky because the Hog Heaven Muzzleloaders of Moscow, Idaho, loaned us two already-made dugouts. We proceeded on with four dugouts down the Clearwater River onto the Snake River and finally onto the Columbia River to the Pacific Ocean.

A dugout canoe is a log, and a log is unstable. Furthermore, the weight of the canoe and its crew give you a low side draft between the gunnel and the water, thus one of our dugouts capsized in the rapids of the Clearwater River. We had dugouts swamp when boaters went by us at full speed. Their wake would fill the dugouts with water, and consequently, swamping would occur. Several times, the dugouts swamped in the swells of the Columbia River. We would have to go to the nearest riverbank and bail out the dugouts to make them useable. It was not unusual to bail out our dugouts in the morning after a rainstorm. The dugouts would fill with rainwater, or sometimes wind-blown waves would fill the dugout canoes. Basically, maintenance on dugout canoes is minimal, but they do require constant bailing in rough water, whether it is natural or manmade.

Upon the 1805 expedition's arrival at Dismal Nitch (near present day Chinook, Washington), the men of the expedition were astounded to see the Indians in canoes that were seaworthy. On the return trip in 1806, the expedition used two of the Chinook-type canoes and two dugout canoes to proceed up the Columbia River to The Dalles.

The Chinook Indians greeted us on our arrival at Station Camp in November of 2005. They gifted us with salmon and gave us permission to make a replica of one of their canoes. Dick Brumley, a member of our organization, made the canoe during the winter of 2005–2006. We used his Chinook canoe replica in our return trip up the Columbia River.

The original expedition abandoned all boats near The Dalles and were on horseback from this point till they recovered six dugout canoes at Camp Fortunate. These are the canoes they left there in August of 1805 when they ran out of water near the headwaters of the Beaverhead River (which becomes the Jefferson River and the Jefferson River eventually becomes the Missouri River).

The original journey from Traveler's Rest to the confluence of the Yellowstone River is quite complicated. I can't believe Captain Lewis divided his forces as he did, but he did. It is worth looking into because the forces ended up using dugout canoes, bullboats, the white pirogue, and a catamaran.

Upon arrival at Traveler's Rest, Captains Lewis and Clark agreed to split their forces for exploration purposes in accordance with President Jefferson's wishes. Captain Lewis would immediately go to the Great Falls area and explore the Maris River area. Captain Clark would follow the trail from last year to the Three Rivers area and explore the Yellowstone River area. They agreed to meet at the confluence of the Yellowstone River, which today is a couple of miles from the Montana–North Dakota state line.

All personnel were on horseback at this time. In 1806, at Traveler's Rest, Captain Lewis had been told by local Indians that the Great Falls were three sleeps away. If Captain Lewis had known this on his travels west, he could have saved about thirty days by bypassing the journey to the headwaters of the Missouri River, crossing the Lemhi Pass, and then following the Bitterroot Valley to Traveler's Rest. But then again, he would not have been following President Jefferson's wishes to find a waterway to the far ocean for the purpose of commerce.

Captain Lewis left Traveler's Rest with nine men. Upon arrival at the Great Falls, he took three men and proceeded north into Maris River country. He left six men at the Great Falls to meet with the men from Captain Clark's group coming down the Missouri River in dugout canoes.

Meanwhile Captain Clark, with twenty-two men and Sacagawea, retraced the Bitterroot Valley trail, crossed over the continental divide in the area of Gibbons Pass, and recovered six dugout canoes at Camp Fortunate. They proceeded down the Missouri River with the dugouts to Three Rivers. Here, Captain Clark sent Sergeant Ordway down the Missouri River with the dugouts and ten men to meet Captain Lewis' men at the Great Falls. Clark took the remaining people over land to the Yellowstone River near today's Big Timber, Montana.

Upon arrival at the Yellowstone River, Captain Clark had two dugout canoes built. He had them lashed together and made a catamaran out of these two canoes. He sent Sergeant Pryor overland with two men to deliver all the horses (forty-nine) to Fort Mandan, and he proceeded down the Yellowstone.

The first night out, all of the horses disappeared (probably stolen). Sergeant Pryor and his men then proceeded to make two bullboats. A bullboat is made by fastening tree limbs or branches together in a circular pattern, and then covering the structure with a hide (usually buffalo). The men had seen this type of a boat when they wintered near the Mandan Indian Villages. They paddled down the Yellowstone in their bullboats until they caught up with Captain Clark. The bullboats and catamaran continued on to the confluence of the Yellowstone River.

Meanwhile, Sergeant Ordway met Sergeant Gass and his six men at the Great Falls. They joined forces, portaged the falls, and recovered the white pirogue near the lower portage camp. The red pirogue was recovered the next day, but it had deteriorated to the point where it was unusable.

Upon recovering the white pirogue, the group proceeded down the Missouri River, met Captain Lewis near the confluence of the Maris River, and met Captain Clark near the confluence of the Yellowstone River.

Our group tried to mirror the original group's travels. We also split our forces. One group headed for the Maris River area, and the other group headed for the Yellowstone River. We also eventually met at the Yellowstone River confluence.

I joined the Yellowstone River group. We proceeded to Camp Fortunate where we launched our dugouts and traveled down the Beaverhead River to Three Rivers, then overland to the Yellowstone River where we launched and lashed our dugouts together and made a catamaran. A catamaran is much more stable than a single dugout and therefore much more fun to paddle. We even burst into song on our way down the Yellowstone and Missouri Rivers as we headed toward Saint Louis and cold beer.

You may ask, "Where are your boats today?" Good question. Our keelboat, two pirogues, and two dugouts are in our boathouse in Saint Charles, Missouri. Two dugouts have been returned to the Missouri Conservation Department, and the last two dugouts have been returned to the Hog Heaven Muzzleloaders of Moscow, Idaho. It was very nice of these organizations to loan us dugouts when we were in their neighborhoods. Just remember, the expedition of 1803–1806 was helped by locals. The Indians traded for or gave the expedition horses, food, boats, information, guides, lodging, and other survival tools. We were no different. The modern-day locals made our journey possible by furnishing us with the same material help, and we are very appreciative of what they have done for us.

The Men and Women

During our travels, we were quite often asked, "How many men were on the expedition at this time, and how many men do you have on the river?" The answer depends on the time frame in which you are speaking. Let's start at the beginning of the expedition in 1803.

When Captain Lewis accepted the keelboat on August 31, 1803, in Pittsburgh, Pennsylvania, from John Walker, he was the only soldier on the boat.

Lewis proceeded to hire several river boatmen (perhaps five or six) to help him load the boat and sail it down the Ohio River.

I have read a United States Army publication that states that seven soldiers were being transferred from Carlisle Barracks, Pennsylvania, to Fort Massac, Indiana Territory (Indiana Territory encompassed Illinois at this time) and were assigned to help Lewis in his endeavor. None of these men were part of the contingent that went to the West Coast.

There is also evidence that John Colter and George Shannon may have joined Lewis at Pittsburgh and eventually did enlist into the army at Clarksville, Indiana. They both traveled to the Pacific Ocean and back.

Upon arrival at Clarksville, Indiana on October 14, 1803, Captain William Clark joined Captain Meriwether Lewis, and it was at this time that the expedition became the Lewis and Clark Expedition. Clark's slave, York, also joined the expedition at this time.

Captain Clark had interviewed and recruited several men before the arrival of Lewis, and with Lewis' approval, they enlisted into the army and joined the expedition. These men were frontier woodsmen, adventurers, single (except for John Shields), and eventually supermen. They were referred to as the "nine young men from Kentucky."

On October 15, 1803, Charles Floyd, George Gibson, brothers Joseph Field and Reubin Field, and John Colter enlisted into the United States Army. On October 19, George Shannon and John Shields enlisted into the Unites States Army, and finally, on October 20, Nathaniel Pryor and William Bratton enlisted into the United States Army.

This now gave Captain Lewis eleven soldiers and one civilian for his expedition.

Upon arrival at Fort Massac, Indiana Territory on November 11, 1803, Captain Lewis accepted volunteers John Newman and Joseph Whitehouse, from Daniel Bissell's infantry company, 1st Infantry Regiment. These two men were the first regular army privates to join the Corps of Discovery.

Lewis also hired George Drouillard as an interpreter at Fort Massac. This now gave Lewis thirteen soldiers and two civilians for the Corps of Discovery.

Drouillard was sent to a fort at South West Point, Tennessee to bring eight men from the 2nd Infantry Regiment for an interview at Camp Dubois, Indiana Territory.

Lewis proceeded on to Fort Kaskaskia, Indiana Territory, arriving there on November 29, 1803. Here he enlisted Sergeant John Ordway and Privates Peter Weiser, Richard Windsor, Patrick Gass, John Boley, and John Collins from Russell Bissell's Company, 1st Infantry Regiment. Lewis also accepted volunteers, John Dame, John Robertson, John Thompson, Ebenezer Tuttle, Isaac White, and Alexander Willard from Captain Amos Stoddard's Company, U.S. Corps of Artillery for the journey. On November 30, Francois Labiche enlisted for the expedition.

This now gave Captain Lewis twenty-six soldiers and two civilians for the adventure. As you can see, Captain Lewis was building his forces as he proceeded on his mission.

Because of the number of men now part of the Corps of Discovery, it was at this point that Lewis determined that he needed an additional boat for the expedition. He requisitioned the white pirogue from the army garrison at Fort Kaskaskie.

On December 12, 1803, the Corps of Discovery arrived at Wood River, Indiana Territory and proceeded to build their winter camp, which was named Camp Dubois.

On December 22, Drouillard arrived from the fort at South West Point, Tennessee with eight men. They were interviewed, and four were sent back to South West Point. The four men who were retained were Corporal Richard Warfington and Privates Thomas Howard, John Potts, and Hugh Hall.

This now gave Lewis thirty soldiers and two civilians for the expedition.

Several other soldiers were added to the corps during the winter months. They were Privates Pierre Cruzatte, Silas Goodrich, Jean Lepage, Hugh McNeal, and Moses Reed.

This now gave Lewis thirty-five soldiers, two civilians, and seven or eight engages for the trip to Fort Mandan.

It was during the stay at Fort Mandan that Captain Lewis hired Toussaint Charbonneau and his wife, Sacagawea, as interpreters. With the Charbonneaus came Jean Baptiste Charbonneau, their two-month-old baby.

At the time of departure from Fort Mandan, on April 7, 1805, Captain Lewis sent the keelboat back to Saint Louis. Corporal Warfington was in charge of its return trip. On board were several soldiers. Two of whom had been court-martialed (Newman and Reed). All of the engages were also sent back to Saint Louis at this time for two reasons: first, they were not soldiers in the United States Army, and this was a military expedition; secondly, their expertise as river boatmen and stevedores was no longer needed. The soldiers remaining on the expedition could properly handle all of the engages' responsibilities.

Getting back to the original question as to how many men were on the expedition, it all depends on where the expedition was located at the time the question was asked. A good number to use going up the Missouri River to the Mandans is forty-five. The final number for the trip from Fort Mandan to the Pacific Ocean and back is thirty-three. Which consisted of twenty-nine soldiers and four civilians, one of whom was a woman and not counting the baby.

During this epic journey only one man died. Sergeant Charles Floyd died on August 20, 1804, near present day Sioux City, Iowa. He apparently died of appendicitis. All the symptoms described in the journals lead the medical profession of today to believe that his cause of death was appendicitis. Appendicitis was not known to the medical profession in 1804. Consequently, there was nothing Captains Lewis or Clark could have done to help Sergeant Floyd. He was buried with full military honors.

Considering all of the hardships, perils, rivers, and animal confrontations encountered by the Corps of Discovery, it is miraculous that only one man died during their journey and that Sergeant Floyd's death was a natural death.

Now for the modern-day men and women on the reenactment.

There were approximately 250 members in the Discovery Expedition of Saint Charles. A manageable number of personnel on the river at any one time was thirty. This would give us about fifteen men on the boat crew and fifteen personnel on the ground crew. I say personnel because, unlike the original expedition, we had quite a few of our women members assisting us on the ground crew. We realize that this was a military expedition and had only one woman on the expedition in the 1803–1806 period. But our women certainly contributed to the success of our mission in the 2003–2006 period.

Again, unlike the original Corps of Discovery, we rotated men on and off the river for three years. This was due to the inability of most of our volunteers to commit to extended periods of time on the river.

Two men probably performed more time on the river than anyone else. They were Bud Clark who portrayed his great-great-great-grandfather, Captain William Clark, and Josh Loftis, who is the great-great-great-great-grandnephew of George Shannon.

As we progressed across the country, we interacted with other organizations who had local members of their organizations portraying certain individuals. When we joined them in their hometown areas, we gladly accepted their reenactors into our ranks. At times our men stepped aside, and we supported the local individuals and their organizations.

Our Discovery Expedition of St. Charles integrated with several of the Lewis and Clark Brigades/Chapters. The most notable were the Sergeant Floyd Brigade in Sioux City, Iowa; the Great Falls Brigade in Great Falls, Montana; the Traveler's Rest Brigade in Lolo, Montana; the Hog Heaven Muzzleloaders in Moscow, Idaho; and the Fort Clatsop Reenactors at Fort Clatsop, Oregon.

Captain Lewis was portrayed by several of our members. The first being Scott Mandrell, a schoolteacher from Alton, Illinois; Bryant Boswell, a dentist from Jackson, Mississippi; Jan Donelson, a businessman from Wildwood, Missouri; and Mike Dotson, a businessman from Monon, Indiana.

Captain Clark was primarily portrayed by Bud Clark, a retired engineer from Dearborn, Michigan, but his cousin, Charles Clark, of Saint Louis, Missouri, ably assisted him, as did Craig "Rocky" Rockwell, a United States Army Corps of Engineers employee of Clarkston, Washington, and David Hommes, Washington, Missouri.

Sergeant Ordway would be a unit's first sergeant in today's army, even though he was not called that in 1803. Over the years, several men portrayed him. The first being Peter Geery, St.Charles, Missouri; then Tom Marshall, St. Louis, Missouri; Gary Ulrich, St. Louis, Missouri; Steve Meyer, Jefferson City, Missouri; Tom Eier, Lewiston, Idaho; and Bob Staton, California, Missouri.

Sergeant Pryor was ably portrayed by Norm Bowers, St. Louis, Missouri; Bill Shansey, Ashland, Missouri; and Vern Illi, Troy, Idaho.

Sergeant Gass was portrayed by Mike Calwell, Mission, Kansas; John Hess, Somerset, California; David Hibbler, St. Charles, Missouri; Paul Rebscher, Moriches, New York; and Andy Janicki, Georgetown, Pennsylvania.

Sergeant Floyd was portrayed by John Fisher, Juliaetta, Idaho, and Steve Everly, Olathe, Kansas, until Sergeant Floyd died. Then they portrayed the "Ghost of Floyd"

York was ably portrayed by Willie Lyles, Liberty, Missouri; Joe Bradford, Eugene, Oregon; Porter Williams, Valley Springs, South Dakota; Lyndon Hart, Watertown, South Dakota; and Julius Udinyiwe, Booneville, Missouri.

We did not have a Sacagawea with us on every day of our trip. But whenever we needed a Sacagawea for a parade, powwow, or other festive event, we had several ladies who ably assisted us. Most notably was Jan "Two Bears" Falcon. A Chippewa Cree from the Turtle Mountain Reservation, she portrayed Sacagawea more than anyone else during our journey. Other women who helped us were Eve Pearlmutter, the Discovery Expedition of Saint Charles' Membership Coordinator; Jessica Grinnell, a Mandan Indian; Jacqueline Wallace, a Lolo, Montana resident; and Amy Mossett, a Mandan Indian who left Fort Mandan with us on April 7, 2005, with a papoose. Whenever we were on an Indian Reservation, we did not force the use of one of our Sacagaweas, and we always welcomed a local resident into our midst. Jessica Grinnell fit this bill perfectly. She helped us when we were in the New Town, North Dakota area because this is the area in which Sacagawea lived before joining the Corps of Discovery.

As the journals did for the men on the original expedition, we should recognize some of our men for their talents and abilities.

Our cooks should be singled out for their outstanding contributions to the success of our venture. Primarily Jim Stanley, Mission, Kansas; Bob Anderson, Maryville, Ohio; Rob Fix, Bruceville, Texas; Kevin Talbot, St. Louis, Missouri; Jack Simmons, Hemet, California; Steve Wicken, Springfield, Missouri; and Lloyd Gower, Armada, Michigan. There were other men who pitched in, as well as the women, and kept a semblance of order in the kitchen tent. We never had a problem with tainted food. On most days, these people prepared three meals a day. There were days when only two meals were necessary because of activities on the river, or the local residents fed us.

Our mechanics, carpenters, and boat engineers should be noted. They include, but are not limited to, Neal Corey, McCook, Nebraska; Gary Ulrich, St. Louis, Missouri; Jim Rasher, St. Peters, Missouri; Walter Gotsch, Oakland, Missouri; Dean Clawson, Ballwin, Missouri; Bob Plummer, Portland, Missouri; Jim King, St. Charles, Missouri; and Ken Altergott, Oconto, Wisconsin.

Just like the 1803–1806 expedition, we also had musicians. Most notably were The Booneslick Strings, comprised of Al Puknat, Joe Tesson, and Ron Beights. Other musicians were Rob Fix, bagpipes; John McNulty, fiddle; Charlie Barber, guitar; David Hovde, dulcimer; Bob Swan, guitar; Bob Plummer, jaw harp; and Mark Johnson, guitar. Many, many times, local residents brought their musical instruments into our camps and serenaded us or joined us in entertainment around our campfires. These campfire gatherings can never be forgotten. They were a once-in-a-lifetime experience. We try to duplicate them whenever we have a gathering, but there is something magical about those nights spent around a campfire while on the river. It is very difficult to put these experiences into words, but the men and women who experienced them will never forget them. It is so sad to see them evaporate.

So much has been written about the men on the original expedition because there were so few of them. The Discovery Expedition of Saint Charles is comprised of many outstanding men and women. As we look at the membership rolls, just remember that our members came and went over a five-year period. To honor all who participated in and supported this reenactment, we must acknowledge all members. As you look through this listing, you will see that thirty-six states are represented. If the individuals' vocations were listed, you would also see the same and probably a more varied assortment of vocations than the members on the 1803–1806 expedition. For purposes of posterity and for the future historians who study our reenactment, this listing of participants gives them some groundwork to work with.

Adams, Chuck—Morgantown, IN

Altergott, David—Oconto, WI

Altergott, Joanne—Oconto, WI

Altergott, Ken—Oconto, WI

Ambrose, Elliot—Jefferson City, MO

Ambrose, William—Jefferson City, MO

Anderson, Gary—Center, ND

Anderson, Jeanne—Lake Ozark, MO

Anderson, John—Carefree, AZ

Anderson Norman—Great Falls, MT

Anderson, Robert—Maryville, OH

Andrew, Ragan—Long Beach, WA

Arnold, Larry—Dayton, OH

Ashcraft, Ken—Loveland, OH

Assman, Edward—Pierre, SD

Aubuchon, Martin—St. Louis, MO

Bachman, Neal—Arkansas City, KS

Bahr, Geoff—Blue Springs, MO

Baker, Mike—Lee's Summit, MO

Ballentine, Scott—Jamestown, IN

Ballentine, Vicki—Jamestown, IN

Barber, Charles—Mandan, ND

Barnhill, Billy—Cahokia, IL

Barron, Bob—Washington, MO

Barry, Doug—Turners Station, KY

Bartholomew, David—Fishers, IN

Bartlett, Marty—Huntington, WV

Bates, Rick—St. Paul, MO

Bechtol, Frank—Taylor, MI

Bechtol, Marvin—Taylor, MI

Beck, Arlen—Davenport, IA

Becker, Ann Marie—St. Louis, MO

Becker, John—Godfrey, IL

Becker, Rex—Fairfax Station, VA

Belt, Greg—Urbana, OH

Benson, David—Onaway, ID

Bergh, Ray—Morgan, UT

Bergman, David—Indianapolis, IN

Bergmann, Nick—Cincinnati, OH

Berkemeyer, Ken—Morrison, MO

Bertolini, Joseph—Waynesville, OH

Berwinkle, Tom—Clarksburg, WV

Bettorf, Athena, Alton, IL

Bettorf, Virgil—Alton, IL

Biddle, Derek—Rocheport, MO

Biffle, Earl—Fenton, MO

Bishop, David—Cynthiana, IN

Bishop, Joanne—St. Charles, MO

Blevins, Dale—Independence, MO

Bolinger, Lewis—So Whitley, IN

Bonafede, Mike—Loveland, CO

Bonde, David—Fort Pierre, SD

Boozer, Jerry—W Chester, OH

Borisov, Alex—St. Charles, MO

Boschen, Larry—Florissant, MO

Boswell, Bryant—Star, MS

Boucher, William—Elizabeth, PA

Bowers, Brigitte—St. Louis, MO

Bowers, Garret—St. Charles, MO

Bowers, Greg—O'Fallon, IL

Bowers, Norman—St. Louis, MO

Bowman, Joyce—Plattsmouth, NE

Bowman, Michael—Plattsmouth, NE

Boyer, James—Winfield, MO

Bradford, Joseph—Eugene, OR

Bragg, John—O'Fallon, MO

Brauner, Paul—Ballwin, MO

Brecht, Bill—St. Charles, MO

Breckenridge, Mark—Ballwin, MO

Bright, Bill—Riverside, MO

Bright, David—Riverside, MO

Bright, Kay—Riverside, MO

Brown, Crosby—Washington, MO

Brown Norman—Newburg, MO

Brown, Vincent—Owensboro, KY

Brumley, Delayne—Lewistown, MT

Brumley, Richard—Lewistown, MT

Bryan, Norman—Jefferson City, MO

Bryant, Doris—Silver Springs, MD

Buckler, William—Hermann, MO

Buckley, Gary—Piedmont, MO

Burke, Ron—Bourbon, MO

Bush, Garry—Lewiston, ID

Butler, Stephen—Defiance, MO

Caffrey, Patrick—New Iberia, LA

Cain, David—Raytown, MO

Calwell, Mike—Mission, KS

Cameron, Scott—Corvallis, MT

Campbell, Dean—Springfield, IL

Campbell, Richard—Jackson, MO

Cardwell, Darlene—Eureka, MO

Carr, Larry—St. Peters, MO

Carroll, Kyle—Maysville, MO

Carter, Greg—Overland, MO

Cave, Shannon—Holts Summit, MO

Champlin, Rita—St. Louis, MO

Champlin, Robert—St. Louis, MO

Cimarosti, John—Cincinnati, OH

Clark, Bud—Dearborn, MI

Clark, Charlie—St. Louis, MO

Clark, Churchill—Aurora, CO

Clark, Dale—Grand Island, NE

Clark, John—Brighton, MI

Clawson, Dean—Ballwin, MO

Clifton, David—Vichy, MO

Clutz, George—Frankfort, SD

Clutz, Greg—Watertown, SD

Clutz, Virgina—Frankfort, SD

Coble, Jay—Rhodes, IA

Colbert, Nick—Madison, IA

Combs, Barney—Arnold, MO

Corder, Eric—Huntington, WV

Corey, Mary Lee—McCook, NE

Corey, Neal—McCook, NE

Crecelius, Burt—Oakland City, IN

Crinkelmeyer, Ollie—Austin, TX

Crouch, Mike—Seymour, IN

Cullen, Charles—Bismarck, ND

Curry, Clark—Edmond, OK

Darcy, John—Yankton, SD

Darlington, Hank—Gold River, CA

Daum, Jon—Leavittsburg, OH

Davis, Eric—Marseilles, IL

Davis, Glenn—Cincinnati, OH

Dawkins, Audrey—Bloomington, IL

Dawkins, Bill—Bloomington, IL

Day, Julie—St.Charles,MO

Dearing, Brian—The Plains, OH

D'LaRonde, Joe—Glorieta, NM

Dempsy, Tom—St. Charles MO

Dengler, John—St. Charles, MO

Dewes, Ed—Bainbridge, IN

Dickinson, Roscoe—Kansas City, MO

Dillon, Rick—Effingham, KS

Dimmick, Dave—Murryville, IL

Dittmer, Russ—Moores Hill, IN

Doeren, Richard—Oconto, WI

Donelson, Jan—Wildwood, MO

Donelson, Tammy—Wildwood, MO

Donnelly, George—Helena, MT

Dostal, Darrell—Potosi, MO

Dostal, Joan—Potosi, MO

Dotson, Mike—Monon, IN

Douglas, Lewis—Eminence, KY

Drullard, Jeff—Stockton, CA

Dubbeld, Walt—Huntington, IN

Dufur, Brett—Rocheport, MO

Duncan, Esther—Veedersburg, IN

Dunn, John—Westwood, KS

Dupre, Patrick—Augusta, MO

Duren, Ralph—Jefferson City, MO

Durney, Jim—St. Charles, MO

Durrett, Deanna—Crawfordsville, IN

Durrett, Robert—Crawfordsville, IN

Eier, Thomas—Lewiston, ID

Eller, Edwin—St. Louis, MO

Engman, Nora—Liberty, MO

Everly, Steve—Olathe, KS

Falcon, Jan Two Bears—Lake Stevens, WA

FalconNeihardt, Joy—Laveen, AZ

Falvo, Ed—Port Vue, PA

Fichtler, Dick—Florence, MT

Filkins, Eric—Industry, PA

Fisher, John—Juliaetta, ID

Fix, Robert—Bruceville, TX

Fleek, Sherman—Quicksburg, VA

Forbes, John—Shawnee, KS

Ford, Bob—Cedarville, OH

Forhell, Fred—Waterloo, IL

Fortunato, Carol—Markleysburg, PA

Foster, Perry—Versailles, MO

Fox, Philip—Rochester, PA

Frazier, Joe—Lewistown, MT

Fredli, Doug—Nebraska City, NE

Freedman, Larry—Rhineback, NY

Fritz, Charles—Billings, MT

Gaffney, Ken—Litchfield, IL

Gaffney, Richard—Jefferson City, MO

Garreau, Lloyd—St.Charles, MO

Garrett, Jerry—St.Louis, MO

Garrison, Dan—Lesterville, MO

Garver, Al—Billings, MT

Gaster, Jermey—Indianola, NE

Gaster, Jim—Indianola, NE

Geery, Marilyn—St. Charles, MO

Geery, Peter—St. Charles, MO

Gerard, Tony—Ullin, IL

Getsinger, Kathy—Louisville, KY

Gilbert, Mark—Rineyville, KY

Goddard, Ron—Owensboro, KY

Goodwin, Joe—Renton, WA

Gotsch, Walter—Oakland, MO

Goularot, William—Wheeler, OR

Gower, Lloyd—Amada, MI

Grimm, Arthur—St. Louis, MO

Groce, Dennis—Point Marion, PA

Gronefield, David—Augusta, MO

Haagenson, Bruce—Billings, MT

Hahn, Herb—Monaco, PA

Hairston, Matt—Belleville, IL

Hamberg, Edward—Alton, IL

Hammonds, Buddy—Phoenix, AZ

Hancock, Denis—Columbia, MO

Hankla, Scott—Frankfort, KY

Hansen, Dave—Fort Pierre, SD

Happle, Chuck—Walsh, IL

Harrington, Tom—Brimfield, MA

Harris, Thomas—Alton, IL

Hart, Lyndon—Watertown, SD

Hasting, Nancy—Mt Vernon, IN

Haurwonds, Claude—Phoenix, AZ

Haynes, Ralph—New Haven, MO

Hebb, James—Wheat Ridge, CO

Hebenstreit, Jerry—St. Louis, MO

Hedges, Gregory—Bridgeville, PA

Hegarty, Joe—Stevensville, MD

Hendrick, Bill—Grafton, IL

Herman, Danny—Diamondale, MI

Hernandez, John—Springfield, MO

Herren, James—Glassport, PA

Hesley, Carole—Ballwin, MO

Hesley, Phil—Ballwin, MO

Hess, John—Somerset, CA

Hibbler, David—St. Charles, MO

Hicks, Steve—Zebulan, GA

Hillman, Curtis—Dothan, AL

Hillyer, Joseph—Williamstown, KY

Hodges, Gale—Clarksburg, MO

Hoffman, Tim—Poseyville, IN

Hodges, Gale—Clarksburg, MO

Holbrook, Tony—Tarlton, OH

Holland, Charles—Marshall, MO

Holton, Eddie—Tombstone, AZ

Hommes, David—Washington, MO

Hopple, Jess—Cape Girardeau, MO

Hoskins, Arlan—Clarinda, IA

Hottes, Larry—Duquoin, IL

Hovde, David—Mulberry, IN

Huber, Eric—Mt Washington, KY

Huber, Harry—Linton, IN

Hughes, David—Freedom, PA

Hughes, Harry—Freedom. PA

Hunt, Joel—Troy, MO

Hunt, Richard—Blair, NE

Husing, Lonnie—Grand Island, NE

Hutsler, Tom—Parkville, MO

Illi, Vern—Troy, ID

Jackson, Darold—St. Charles, MO

Jackson, Mimi—St. Charles, MO

Jackson, Skip—Cincinnati, OH

Jacobs, Jim—Lafayette, IN

Janicki, Andrew—Georgetown, PA

Johnson, Jerry—Hamilton, OH

Johnson, Mark—Portland, OR

Johnston, James—Nebraska City, NE

Jones, Moose,—Portsmouth, OH

Jones, Randy—Alton, IL

Jones, Sharon—Alton, IL

Jurgella, David—Myersville, MD

Kalina, Kenneth—Mokeesport, PA

Kearns, Grant—Marysville, OH

Keen, Lincoln—Calloo, MO

Keeven-Franke, Dorris—Washington, MO

Keller, Warren—Lebanon, IL

Kennedy, Karol—Milford, OH

Kestermeier, Kurt—St. Louis, MO

Kilmer, Robert—Hannibal, MO

Kimbrell, Jordan—Liberty, MO

King, Jim—St.Charles, MO

Kirkland, David—St. Charles, MO

Kirkman, Tom—Avoca, IN

Kirnan, Kevin—Celina, OH

Kluesner, Betty—St. Louis, MO

Kluesner, Larry—St. Louis, MO

Knott, Christina—Smithville, MO

Knott, DeWayne—Smithville, MO

Knowles, Charles—Moscow, ID

Koenders, Greg—Sioux Falls, SD

Krebs, Alvin—Forsythe, MT

Laidlaw, Tom—Vancover, WA

Lake, Richard—Grover, MO

Lammers, Perry—Chicago, IL

Lanahan, C.J.—Troy, IL

Lander, Carl—W Newton, PA

Lange, Philo—Indianapolis, IN

Learned, Bob—St. Louis, MO

LeBlanc, Michael—Cincinnati, OH

LeBrun, Rene—Henderson, AR

LeClaire, Gary—Fenton, MO

Lenoch, William—Spokane, WA

Lentz, Gary—Dayton, WA

LeSage, Richard—Ballwin, MO

Linter, Albert—Wellsville, KS

Lizzo, John—St. Louis, MO

Lockwood, Charles—Columbia, MO

Loftis, Josh—Lake Ozark, MO

Louderback, Ron—Felicity, OH

Love, Rolland—Overlook Park, KS

Lucy, Gary—Washington, MO

Ludington, Harry—Farmington, IL

Luebben, Tom—Belleville, IL

Luer, Carol—Maryland Heights, MO

Lyles, Willie—Liberty, MO

Mac Swain, Travis—Pensacola, FL

Magee, Rick—Royalston, MA

Magnuson, Kris—Ilwaco, WA

Magrath, Joseph—Santa Fe, NM

Maitz, Doug—Clarkson Valley, MO

Mandrell, Scott—Alton, IL

Marguet, Joe—Greenville, IN

Marshall, Tom—St. Louis, MO

Martin, Jack—Chaffee, MO

Martin, John—Kansas City, MO

Maxheimer, Greta—St. Louis, MO

Mayden, David—Lake St. Louis, MO

McClain, Larry—St. Charles, MO

McCutchen, Daryl—Cincinnati, OH

McKee, Pete—Chester, VA

McKinney, Frank—Missoula, MT

McNulty, John—Pittsburgh, PA

Meehan, Joanne—University City, MO

Meeks, David—St. Charles, MO

Messick, Mike—Kansas City, MO

Metzidakis, Stamos—Clayton, MO

Meyer, John—Kansas City, MO

Meyer, Richard—Haubdtadt, IN

Meyer, Stephen—Jefferson City, MO

Michael, Larry—Farmington, MO

Midkiff, Bruce—Ambridge, PA

Miller, Bud—Clarkston, WA

Miller, Chris—Jefferson City, MO

Miller, David—Cortland, NY

Miller, Margaret—Cathlamet, WA

Miller, Richard—Jefferson, City, MO

Mitchell, Jean—Seattle, WA

Mohler, David—St. Louis, MO

Mollison, James—Pierre, SD

Monckton, Jan—Rocheport, MO

Montgomery, Mike—Henley, MO

Moore, Michael—Great Falls, VA

Morrell, Lynn—St.Charles, MO

Morris, Gary—Fair Grove, MO

Morris, Robert—Finleyville, PA

Mott, David—Olathe, KS

Mueller, Ted—Chester, IL

Muich, Doug—St. Louis, MO

Mullins, Art—Beaver, OH

Murphy, Jesse—Billings, MT

Murphy, Sam—Kearney, MO

Murray, Pete—Burbank, SD

Nash, Tim—Thorn Town, IN

Nelson, Benjamin—Omaha, NE

Nelson, Eric—Ilwaco, WA

Nelson, Len—Ilwaco, WA

Nicholson, Tom—St. Louis, MO

Niemeier, Jerry—Harrisburg, MO

Niemeier, Zack—Harrisburg, MO

Norman, Bryan—Jefferson City, MO

Nuckles, Steven—Bridgeville, PA

O'Brien, Danny—Grandview, MO

O'Brien, Patrick—St. Louis, MO

O'Dell, John—Harrisburg, IL

Oloteo, Dennis—O'Fallon, MO

Olsen Clifford—Jefferson City, MO

Osborn Tom, Flat Rock, IL

Overbey, Bruce—Columbia, IL

Oxley, Charles—Cape Girardeau, MO

Padgett, Bob—Manhattan Beach, CA

Parrott, Greg—Robinson, IL

Payne, Jerry—Bainbridge, OH

Pearlmutter, Eve—Wright City, MO

Pecoraro, Robert—Jennings, MO

Peterson, Paul—Louisville, KY

Pierce, Michael—Cairo, MO

Piotrowski, Clement—Brookport, IL

Plummer, Mike—Washington, MO

Plummer, Robert—Portland, MO

Porter, John—Clayton, MO

Potts, Ryan—Braddyville, IA

Prestholdt Elaine—Bridgewater, NJ

Prestholdt, Richard—Bridgewater, NJ

Puchany, Fred—Cannonsburg, PA

Puknat, Al—Arnold, MO

Pullum, Linda—Gray Summit, MO

Quinby, Abram—Bear, DE

Ramsey, Howard—Keyesport, IL

Rasher, Jim—St. Peters, MO

Rebscher, Paul—Moriches, NY

Reeves, John—St. Charles, MO

Reid, Jim—St. Charles, MO

Reising, Keith—Columbus, IN

Rhine, Everett—Anna, IL

Rhodes, Richard—Dayton, OH

Richey, Michael—Columbia, MO

Riley, Jim—St. Charles, MO

Ripley, Peter—Mokane, MO

Roberts, Rick—Lewisburg, TN

Robertson, Dennis—Lexington, KY

Rock, Gerry—Santa Fe, NM

Rockwell, Craig—Clarkston, WA

Roeder, Jim—Silvis, IL

Ronk, Tom—Jefferson City, MO

Rose, Bill—Charolette, NC

Rosenberger, Jim—Verona, WI

Rotkin, Lance—Indianapolis, IN

Rumelhart, Randy—Burbank, SD

Ruybalid, Jon—Lincoln, VA

Saathoff, Brian—Arthur, IL

Saathoff, William—Gregory, SD

Sallade, Marianne—Bellvue, NE

Sartorius, Dr Gregg—St. Peters, MO

Sartorius, Michael—St. Peters, MO

Sauer, Matt—Bellbrook, OH

Schiefer, Sandra—Fallbrook, CA

Schneider, Sue—St. Charles, MO

Scholl, Ed—Philadelphia, PA

Schroyer, Chuck—Pierre, SD

Schryver, William—St. Louis, MO

Schulz, Gene—Beavercreek, OH

Seigla, Carl—Goshen, OH

Shansey, William—Ashland, MO

Shaw, Fred—Milford, OH

Shell, William—Sikeston, MO

Shurr, Donald—North Liberty, IA

Silvestri, Richard—Jensen Beach, FL

Simmons, Jack—Hemet, CA

Sindelar, Jeffery—Wildwood, MO

Singleton, Warren—Sedalia, CO

Slosberg, Daniel—Los Angeles, CA

Slow, Randall—Wood River, IL

Slusser, Richard—Chamois, MO

Smith, Dale—Kansas City, MO

Smith, Donald—Santa Fe, NM

Smith, Jim—Greensburg, PA

Smith, Russel—Cedar Rapids, IA

Sonnenfeld, Jim—Centerville, VA

Spainhour, Jeff—Clarksville, IN

Speck, Ellen—Gann Vallry, SD

Spisak, Lawrence—Morgantown, WV

Sprague, Hugh—Jefferson City, MO

Sprague, Sally—Jefferson City, MO

Stanley, Jim—Mission, KS

Stasiak, Noel—St. Louis, MO

Staton, Bob—California, MO

Steadman, Norman—Weippe, ID

Stevens, Kelly—Hermann, MO

Stewart, Bill—Lansing, KS

Stiegemeier, Barbara—St. Charles, MO

Stites, Tim—St. Joseph, MO

Stober, Ed—Milford, OH

Stoffels, Sidney—Garden Valley, CA

Stone, Jack—Marthasville, MO

Stone, Monty—St. Charles, MO

Strater, Roger—W Lafayette, IN

Strum, Jim—Ballwin, MO

Sullivan, Jack—St. Louis, MO

Swan, Bob—Lawrence, KS

Swanson, Craig—Denver City, TX

Swanson, James—Sioux City, IA

Talbot, Kevin—St. Louis, MO

Taylor, Don—Labadie, MO

Tesson, Joe—Warrenton, MO

Teuschler, Julia—Versailles, KY

Thomas, Edward—Decatur, NE

Thompson, Laura—St. Louis, MO

Thurston, Darrell—Pulaski, IL

Tichacek, Allen—Labadie, MO

Tichacek, Dr Cyndy—Labadie, MO

Tilford, Kenneth—Edwardsville, KS

Tofte, Connie—Williston, ND

Tofte, David—Williston, ND

Tomko, Lucinda—Chicago, IL

Townsend, Buddy—Muncie, IN

Trader, Patrick—Paris, KY

Trotter, Lynette—Lansing, KS

Troupe, Jeffery—Oakland, NE

Truppi, George—Lake Stevens, WA

Tucker, Jim—Kansas City, MO

Tyler, Thomas—St. Louis, MO

Udinyiwe, Julius—Booneville, MO

Ulrich, Gary—St. Louis, MO

Ulrich, Nancy—St. Louis, MO

Unsold, Doug—Waterford, OH

Urbanowicz, John—St. Charles, MO

Vance, Louis—San Antonio, TX

Vantol, Larry—Wentzville, MO

Vargo, David—Bethel Park, PA

Viessman, John—Vienna, MO

Vodisek, Lisa—Larua, IL

Vogan, Chuck—New Brighton, PA

Waldo, Clyde—New Florence, MO

Waldo, Ellen—New Florence, MO

Walker, Walt—Great Falls, MT

Wallace, Jim—Cereal Springs, IL

Watson, Dean—Linton, IN

Weaver, Roger—Switz City, IN

Weber, Stanley—Longview, WA

Webster, David—Farmington, MO

Wells, Forest—Owensboro, KY

Weitzien, Alec—Dillon, MT

Wendlick, Roger—Portland, OR

Werner, Jim—Verona, WI

Wesley, Frank—Bonnots, MO

West, Lee—Jefferson City, MO

Westerfield, William—Evansville, IN

Weston, Patricia—Rockwood, PA

Whalen, Ned—St. Louis, MO

Wicken Steve—Brookline, MO

Wilding, Harry—Jefferson City, MO

Williams, Aubrey—Brazil, IN

Williams, Porter—Valley Springs, SD

Williams, Tom—Temperance, MI

Willis, Jim—Union, KY

Wills, Tim—Farley, MO

Wilson, Jerry—Versailles, IN

Wilson, Tom—London, OH

Windland, Harry—Glen Carbon, IL

Wright, Donald—Mound City, MO

Wright, Russ—Maysville, MO

Wurtz, Kevin—Elk Point, SD

Wyatt, Steven—Jefferson City, MO

Young, Douglas—Perry, KS

Young, Bill—Columbia, MO

Young, Doug—Perry, KS

Young, Tom—Ridgeway, MO

The First Leg of Four

August 31 to December 12, 2003

We were on the rivers for sixteen weeks during this leg of our journey. Upon leaving Elizabeth, Pennsylvania, we traveled twenty-two miles down the Monongahela River, 973 miles down the Ohio River, and 195 miles up the Mississippi River to Wood River, Illinois, and Camp Dubois.

We had the luxury of our phase leaders coordinating our stops with mayors, tribal representatives, directors of bicentennial committees, coordinators of local historical societies and tourism offices, representatives of the National Park Service, the National Guard, the United States Army Corps of Engineers, the National Lewis and Clark Bicentennial Commission, the Lewis and Clark Trail Heritage Foundation, and many other organizations and individuals who had an interest in a successful reenactment of the 1803–1806 Lewis and Clark Expedition.

Some of these visits were made a year ahead of our arrival dates. We asked the visiting communities for four items. First was water for drinking and cooking, then firewood for cooking and our nightly campfires, then restrooms, and finally showers. We also inquired about the locations for our tents, availability of straw for ground cover for our tents, laundry facilities, parking for our vehicles, religious entities (for Sundays), the number of schoolchildren who will be visiting our camp, and a myriad of other questions.

These visits also gave our phase leaders an opportunity to survey the docking facilities for our boats. Some communities had piers and docks available for docking. When these facilities were not available, our phase leaders had to make a determination as to the best area for a riverbank landing.

As a result of this coordination, we were able to assist the local communities with their plans for ceremonies, parades, powwows, television, press coverage, and any other initiatives they desired.

We tried to follow the journals in seeking campsites. The rivers and their banks have changed in 200 years, and some of the original campsites are now under water or on private property. Many landowners were very cooperative when it became known that we were recognizing the historical significance of their property and gave us permission to use the campsite on their property. Local historical societies were also very helpful in finding campsites near the original campsites. But, alas, some original campsites are under macadamized parking lots, buildings, and warehouses near the rivers. Some communities and cities have waterfront parks that commemorate Lewis and Clark's visit(s) to their communities. These locations were readily made available to us for our campsites. Consequently, we were able to complete all stops on our planned schedule.

August 31 was the date we left Elizabeth, Pennsylvania. Prior to our departure, members of the Mandan-Hidatsa-Arikara community were on the dock and blessed our boat. They also asked the Great Spirit to keep us safe on our journey. For the next three years, Native Americans, as they are referred to east of the Mississippi River, or Indians, as they are called west of the Mississippi River, were an integral part of our journey. No disrespect is intended by using the word Indian(s). They call themselves Indians and are proud of it. Rightly so! We met dozens and dozens of tribes on our journey. Many of them gifted us, and we responded appropriately. It is no secret that the Lewis and Clark Expedition changed Indian culture forever. Our reenactment made every effort to try to heal some of the wounds that may still persist today. We listened to their grievances and gave the Indians a platform to voice these grievances. All in all, our meetings with Indian chiefs and elders were very congenial and always contained a spirit of friendliness. This was exhibited by the Indian participation in our departing ceremony in Elizabeth, Pennsylvania, and then at Clarksville, Indiana, on October 22, when members of the Shawnee Tribe hosted us for a dinner. We were warmly welcomed into their camp. They gifted us, and we reciprocated. Venison stew and other Indian staples were served at the meal. Then we were invited to participate in tomahawk competition, which is also known as a "hawk throw." We were given a pendent to fly from our mast, which guaranteed safe passage through their territory. Incidents like this were not unusual for the remainder of our journey. When we finished our journey and arrived in St. Louis on September 23, 2006, we had Chief Sheheke and his family with us. Consequently, American Indians were with us at the beginning, during, and at the end of our journey.

The following table outlines the location of the original expedition during this leg of our journey. It must be remembered that in 1803 the states of Indiana, Illinois, and Missouri did not exist as states. Indiana and Illinois were part of the Indiana Territory, and Missouri was west of the Mississippi River. Consequently, Missouri was a part of the Louisiana Purchase. The table also indicates the Discovery Expedition of St. Charles's planned schedule for 2003. We made all forty-eight stops, thanks to the coordination of our phase leaders and with the help of all of the communities involved.

Recorded 1803	Planned 2003	River	Miles
	Aug 23–31 Elizabeth, PA	Monongahela	22
Aug 31 Pittsburgh, PA	Aug 31 Fort Pitt, PA	Ohio	0.0
Sep 1 Neville Island, PA	Sep 1–4 Rochester, PA	Ohio	25.0
Sep 2 Hog Island (Beaver County), PA			
Sep 3 Beaver, PA			
Sep 4 Georgetown, PA	Sep 4–6 Fort Steuben, OH	Ohio	67.0
Sep 6 Steubenville, OH	Sep 6 Wellsburg, WV (Visit Sgt Gass' Gravesite, 2 hrs)	Ohio	74.0
Sep 7 Wellsburg	Sep 6–9 Wheeling, WV	Ohio	90.0
Sep 8 Wheeling			
Sep 9 Bellair, OH	Sep 9–10 Sistersville, OH	Ohio	137.0
Sep 10 Clairington,OH	Sep 10–13 Marietta, OH	Ohio	172.0
Sep 11 Traveled 26 miles			
Sep 12 Mill Creek Island			

Sep 13 Marietta, OH	Sep 13–15 Belpre,OH	Ohio	184.5
Sep 14 Parkersburg			
Sep 15 Hocking River	Sep 15–17 Ravenswood, WV	Ohio	220.7
Sep 16 Traveled 19 miles			
Sep 17 Traveled 7 miles	Sep 17–19 Gallipolis, OH	Ohio	269.1
Sep 18 Letart Falls, OH	Sep 19–21 Huntington, WV	Ohio	308.1
	Sep 21–23 W Portsmouth, OH	Ohio	363.0
	Sep 23–24 Maysville, KY	Ohio	408.7
	Sep 24–25 Augusta, KY	Ohio	427.0
	Sep 25–26 Point Pleasant, OH	Ohio	445.5
Sep 28 Cincinnati, OH	Sep 26–30 New Richmond, OH	Ohio	450.0
	Sep 30–Oct 3 Cincinnati, OH	Ohio	472.0
Oct 4–6 Big Bone Lick, KY	Oct 3–5 Covington, KY	Ohio	474.0

	Oct 5–8 Big Bone Lick State Park, KY	Ohio	516.8
	Oct 8–9 Warsaw, OH	Ohio	528.0
	Oct 9–11 Carrollton, KY	Ohio	545.9
	Oct 11–14 Bethlehem, IN	Ohio	574.9
Oct 14–26 Falls of the Ohio	Oct 14–19 Louisville, KY	Ohio	604.0
	Oct 19–27 Clarksville, IN	Ohio	606.0
Oct 27 West Point, KY	Oct 27–28 West Point, KY	Ohio	630.0
Oct 28 Wyandotte Woods			
Oct 29 Alton	Oct 29–30 Alton, IN	Ohio	679.0
Oct 30 Derby			
Nov 1 Lewisport, KY	Oct 31–Nov 2 Stevensport, KY	Ohio	701.0
Nov 2 Owensboro, KY	Nov 2–3 Owensboro, KY	Ohio	752.0
Nov 4 Evansville	Nov 3–5 Evansville, IN	Ohio	793.0

Nov 5 Mt Vernon	Nov 5–7 Henderson, KY	Ohio	802.0
Nov 7 Old Shawneetown	Nov 7–8 Mt Vernon, IN	Ohio	829.0
Nov 8 Cave-in-Rock	Nov 8–9 Old Shawneetown, IL	Ohio	881.0
	Nov 9–10 Golconda, IL	Ohio	902.0
	Nov 10–12 Paducha, KY	Ohio	935.0
Nov 11–13 Fort Massac	Nov 12–15 Fort Massac, IL	Ohio	939.0
Nov 17–20 Mouth of the Ohio	Nov 15–19 Cairo, IL	Ohio	973.0
	Nov 18–19 Charleston, MO	Mississippi	
	Nov 19–21 Commerce, MO	Mississippi	39.5
Nov 23 Cape Girardeau	Nov 21–24 Cape Girardeau, MO	Mississippi	52.0
	Nov 24–27 Shawnee National Forest	Mississippi	81.5
Nov 29 Fort Kaskaskie	Nov 27–30 Chester, IL	Mississippi	110.0

Nov 30–Dec 1 St Genevieve	Nov 30–Dec 2 Fort Kaskaskie, IL	Mississippi	117.0
	Dec 2–4 St Genevieve, MO	Mississippi	123.0
	Dec 4–6 Fort De Chartres, IL	Mississippi	132.2
Dec 7–9 Cahokia	Dec 6–10 Cahokia, IL	Mississippi	169.0
	Dec10–12 Choteau Island	Mississippi	180.0
Dec 12 Wood River	Dec 12 Camp River Dubois Wood River, IL	Mississippi	195.0

During our travels in leg one, we were provided with some of the necessities of life by the people living along the rivers we traveled on. We were also in touch with the twenty-first century via our laptop computers. Consequently, our followers had many questions about our experiences. A woman had sent an e-mail to us asking about the basics of living on the river. I responded with the following information for her.

Molly:

I spoke with you in Old Shawneetown. I did not know your name at that time, but you did tell me that you had come from Charleston to see the Corp of Discovery II. In our discussion, you were very interested in the overall exploits of our adventure. Our discussion was far too short to give you all the details of our trip. So let's fill you in on some of our meals, shelter, personal hygiene, and the entertainment we are experiencing.

Before we start, I would like to say that I am retired military and share a camaraderie and a bonding with other soldiers that is not found in our normal society. I believe this comes from the fact that my life is in the hands of the soldiers on each side of me and their life is in my hands when we are in harm's way. I mention this because you can see this same bonding with the members of the 1803–1806 expedition. There is no way the 1803–1806 Expedition could have succeeded with out these men trusting each other without question. In the eyes of the military this is discipline, but in the eyes of the individuals this is survival. I have been advised that about 87 percent of the men on our expedition have military service in their background. Consequently, these members of the Corps of Discovery II have a mutual camaraderie for a successful mission. I also sense this feeling in the men who do not have military experience.

Someone once said that an army travels on its stomach. How true—how true. Our cooks provide us with good meals while we are encamped when the locals do not feed us. I mention locals because the 1803–1806 expedition was fed quite often by locals and many Native Americans while on their journey. This food was furnished gratuitously or by bartering or trading.

While on the boats we do not stop for lunch, so you either eat what you have in your haversack (also known as a "possible bag" because anything possible could be found in it), or eat the food in the barrels on the boats. There are three barrels of dried foods on the boats. One has beef jerky or Slim Jims. The second has dried fruit, which consists of dried apples, cranberries, and apricots (I think). The third is filled with parched corn. All of this is nourishing survival food.

I believe that about 70 percent of our meals were furnished or catered by the locals. During my six weeks on the river (not all at one time), I remember a lady in Elizabeth, Pennsylvania who gave us thirty or forty Pennsylvania trout her husband had caught. Our cooks did a fine job on that meal. The people in Rochester, Pennsylvania had a pig roast for us. That pig fed us for two days. In Georgetown, Pennsylvania (population 194) there were two churches side by side, and the local residents had erected a rather large tent between the churches for us. Then the ladies of the two churches brought out their grand- mother's recipes for all kinds of casseroles, chicken dishes, and deserts. What a meal! We were furnished with enough food to last us a week. But alas, we were only there overnight.

Pittsburgh, Pennsylvania, had a spaghetti dinner for us as did Steubenville, Ohio. The friendly people of Wellsburg, West Virginia, gave us a meal after we visited Patrick Gass' grave. We were spoiled in Bethlehem, Indiana. We camped on a man's front yard, and he fed us all of our meals for three days. We ate on his patio. The meals included filet mignon, pork loin, and gourmet breakfasts.

The folks in Louisville invited us to a beast feast. At a beast feast, you are normally served venison, elk, buffalo, turkey, and salmon. Some beast feasts are more exotic and serve such things as rabbit, squirrel, and raccoon. Following our first beast feast, we were invited to about a half dozen more beast feasts at various locations. We were in Clarksville, Indiana, for about eight days and did not cook a meal (well maybe a breakfast or two). The locals took turns catering all of our meals. One day the local rotary club provided dinner, a Subway shop sent us about thirty hoagies for lunch, a Domino's Pizza sent us anoth- er lunch, the Southern Indiana Tourist Office sent us another dinner, a church provided another meal, and a local family was so wrapped up with Lewis and Clark that they had to cook a homemade meal for us. At this point, we could have missed a meal or two and not even noticed.

Old Shawneetown, Illinois, gave us chits for a meal at the food tent next door to us and gave us a beast feast that eve- ning in their historic hotel. Paducah, Kentucky, was another beast feast at the elks and breakfast in their historical soci- ety's building. During our three days at Fort Massac, we were fed all of our meals by the locals. Mothers of the expedition members shouldn't worry about their little boys not eating well, but they should worry about them coming home bigger than when they left. As you can see, we are eating our way across the country.

One last point about eating. Deer hunting season was open in several states that we visited, and half a dozen people gave us venison roasts and shoulders. This includes one of our own members who killed a deer with a bow and arrow, and another one with his flintlock rifle. As did the 1803–1806 expedition, we were living off the land.

As for shelter, we either slept on the boats or in tents. The corps tents are pitched each time we make an encampment. There are three corps tents, and not all of them are pitched every night; only those that are needed. Five men can sleep in a corps tent. Some men pitch their own tents. It is not unusual to have as many as ten tents up at one time. These include the kitchen tent, the store tent, and the orderly room tent. The stressful part about sleeping in a tent is the rain. The boats are tented in such a way as to keep the men on board from sleeping under the stars. A line is rigged amid ship, and a canvas tarp is thrown over the line and then over the side of the boat. This makes a little tent on board the boats. During warm weather, some of the men prefer to sleep under the stars. There are times when we are able to sleep inside. Forts Stuben and Massac presented these opportunities. It is really nice to have a roof over your head and a floor under you. At Fort Massac, we were six or seven to a room—rather crowded. On the last morning, Captain Lewis said that it was like sleeping in a tuberculosis ward, with all the coughing, wheezing, gurgling, snorting, throat clearing, and teeth grinding all night. A new snoring champion was crowned at Fort Massac.

As for showers, we take them whenever the opportunity presents itself. In Elizabeth, Pennsylvania, a resident took three reenactors at a time to his home to let us use his shower. At Pittsburgh, Pennsylvania, we could use a shower located in the museum next to where we camped. In Rochester, Pennsylvania, we were camped within walking distance of the sewage treatment plant and the guys operating the plant let us use their shower. In Wheeling, West Virginia, we were camped next to the Wheeling Arena, which is the home of their local ice hockey team, and we were allowed to use the visiting team's locker room for showers. In Louisville, Kentucky, the corps paid for two hotel rooms, and we were able to use the showers in the hotel. In Clarksville, Indiana, the Southern Indiana Tourist Association let us use the showers that were located in the basement of their historic tollgate building. In Old Shawneetown, Illinois, the junior high school showers were opened for us. In Paducah, Kentucky, the city of Paducah paid for a hotel room for the corps, and we could use this room for showers. At Fort Massac, the campgrounds showers were available for showers. I am sure that I have omitted some other gracious offers for showers, but this list will give you an idea of how the locals are assisting the corps in their journey.

Entertainment is sporadic. There are several members of the corps that play musical instruments, and they are very entertaining when on the river. The most notable of these are The Booneslick Strings. In Elizabeth, Pennsylvania, the local cinema was showing a Lewis and Clark movie, and anyone in uniform was admitted free. The guys in the Elizabeth City Maintenance Department built a big bonfire on a lot next to our encampment each night and had a barrel of beer for our use. On the last two nights in Elizabeth, they brought in their local rock and roll band and gave us free music. Louisville, Kentucky, invited us to a period ball preceded by period dance instructions the night before. The New Albany Indiana High School presented a play titled "Lewis and Clark: The American Journey" while we were in the area. It was free for reenactors. We were brought up on stage before the performance and recognized for our endeavors. It was a very moving experience. The play was outstanding for a high school presentation.

Old Shawneetown, Illinois, put on a local show with local talent that was quite entertaining. It covered the early settlement of their part of Illinois. The Veterans' Day fireworks display at Fort Massac was a show to behold. The half hour presentation should not take a back seat to any other Veterans' Day displays. It was outstanding. I have only covered the time that I have been on the river. I am sure that other forms of entertainment have been offered to the corps, but unfortunately, I have not been privy to their presentations. Naturally, local pubs and taverns have provided aid and comfort to corps members.

We have spilled blood twice on this trip that I know of. The first time was at Patrick Gass's cemetery ceremony. One of our members got his hand caught in his flintlock and ended up bleeding quite profusely. He was marching from the ceremony with blood dripping from his hand. The other incident occurred when one of our members cut off the tip of his thumb. I think it took eight stitches to put him back together. I offered both of these men a Purple Heart Medal, but they both said, "No. Don't belittle this award by such an act of stupidity."

The crew has now been on the river for eleven weeks and has traveled twenty-two miles down the Monongahela River and 973 miles down the Ohio River. They have turned the corner and will be traveling 195 miles up the Mississippi River to Camp DuBois, Wood River, Illinois. I plan to join them again at Fort Kaskaskia, Illinois, where they will pick up the white pirogue. This will give the expedition a third boat. Consequently, a larger boat crew will be needed. I feel honored and privileged to be a part of this historic adventure and look forward to being a part of this journey for the next three years.

—Ed Scholl as Private Hugh Hall,
a fellow Pennsylvanian

Upon her receiving this information, it quickly generated more questions. I answered some of these questions with the following e-mail.

Molly:

There are about 250 reenactors on this expedition. Each one has their own reasons and personal choices for joining the Corps. Consequently, you will need about 250 responses to answer some of your questions. I, for one, am retired military and therefore every day is a vacation day. Two years ago, I took an eighteen-day guided tour with forty-two other people. We traveled from St. Charles, Missouri to Fort Clatsop, Oregon and saw all of the highlights of the original expedition. When I saw what these men and a woman had done and what they had seen, I had to get involved. I surfed the Internet and found that the Discovery Expedition of St. Charles, Missouri was planning to duplicate this monumental journey. I had to get involved. I contacted them and they said, "Welcome. We can use some help." Since this was a military expedition, it was right down my alley. So, here I am.

We are only allowed on the river for two or three weeks at a time (except for a handful of members, for continuity purposes). This is to give the other reenactors a chance to be on the river. Plus, it is very stressful sleeping in tents on the ground in rain and cold weather. For health reasons and peace of mind, it is recommended that a break be taken from these stresses. There are also the physical exertions of moving the camp thirty-nine times during this leg of our trip. Try pitching corps tents and taking them down thirty-nine times. There are about twenty-five reenactors on the river at any one time. These men are divided evenly between a boat crew and a ground crew. Naturally, the boat crew sail the boats, and every man gets a chance at the helm. With enough time at the helm, you can become a boat commander. The ground crew moves the tents and vehicles to the next encampment. The first sergeant usually works out the details for a daily assignment. He tries to put you on the boat one day and on the ground crew the next day. As long as everyone is treated fairly, there is no talk about a mutiny.

As for training, everyone has to undergo a safety orientation before sailing the boats. This includes a man overboard drill, helm usage, line usage and storage, oaring procedures, polling procedures, sailing procedures, cordelling, knowing starboard from port side, and river navigation among other things. Yes, we are soldiers sailing boats. A unique experience as did the 1803–1806 expedition experience. Just remember, that expedition did not have a ground crew. They were truly supermen and a superwoman.

—Ed Scholl as Private Hugh Hall,
a fellow Pennsylvanian

All of these explanations were given and other questions were answered over and over again by our crewmembers whenever we were visited by schoolchildren and interested visitors to our camp-sites. One of our mission mandates was to educate the public on the historical significance and the adventures of the Lewis and Clark 1803–1806 Expedition.

This leg of our journey ended at Wood River, Illinois. Wood River is directly across the Mississippi River from the confluence of the Missouri River. The captains could not place a winter camp on the west bank of the Mississippi River because that territory was not part of the United States. It was in Wood River that C. J. Lanahan of Troy, Illinois, almost singlehandedly built our Camp Dubois to the specifications found in the journals. His labor of love took almost three years.

When we arrived at Camp Dubois on December 12, we put the finishing touches on the camp by covering the roofs with sod and erecting the palisades.

While in Pittsburgh, Pennsylvania, Captain Lewis bought a Newfoundland breed of dog for twenty dollars and named him Seaman. To be historically correct, we also had a Newfoundland dog named Seaman on our reenactment.

A day or two after we arrived at Camp Dubois, it snowed. We were lucky to have a floor under our feet and a roof over our head. Seaman was invited into our huts, but at times, he chose to remain outside.

After the palisades were erected the camp was more like a fort, but it was still referred to as a camp. There are four huts, one on each corner of the camp. Therefore, each mess or squad had its own hut. The fourth hut was a storage hut. There is a large building in the center of the camp that housed the captains' quarters and the hospital.

It was a very pleasant adventure sharing the huts with our crew for a few days.

The interior of the huts had a large room for the sergeant. This room was also used as an orderly/dining/meeting room. The second room had four double bunks for the privates. Actually, the huts were quite cozy and livable.

After dark, the interior of the hut was quite dark, since candles were the only source of light. It was at this time that a phrase was generated, and it subsequently dominated the night hours. The phrase was, "Drink more beer and burn the boxes." As a beer box burns, there is an amazing amount of light and heat for twenty-two seconds. Consequently, you can see who is in the room and sitting across from you. Fortunately, this phrase followed us for the next three years and is still in use today.

The phrase was so popular that the Soho Tavern in Wood River, Illinois saved empty beer boxes for us. After a festive night at the Soho, our group would carry a dozen or so boxes back to camp for use on another night. We were so appreciative of their efforts that we generated a ceiling tile for the Soho, and it can be seen today over the bar in their ceiling. Captain Clark may have carved his name on Pompey's Pillar, but we left our mark on many ceilings, walls, and other tavern paraphernalia, as requested by the owners of these establishments. Our legacy has been preserved for as long as these buildings stand and then some because historical documentation is quite often removed before a building is renovated or raised.

Only one of our men stayed the entire winter at Camp Dubois. He was Bob Anderson of Maryville, Ohio. The rest of us went home and reassembled in May 2004. This is the only time someone from the Discovery Expedition of St. Charles stayed for the winter at one of the original winter encampments.

Fort Mandan is part of the North Dakota State Park system, and since we were not state employees, we could not stay in Fort Mandan for the winter. There was some sort of liability insurance problem. Besides that, I was not too anxious to spend a winter in a primitive encampment in North Dakota.

Unfortunately, Fort Clatsop, Oregon burned to the ground in October 2005. This was just prior to our arrival in November. The cause of the fire was accidental since a friendly fire became a hostile fire when embers apparently sparked out of an open fireplace. The fort has since been rebuilt, thanks to the assistance of many concerned people and organizations in the Astoria, Oregon area.

These first sixteen weeks on the river were a tune-up for what was to come. We literally had our feet wet and crewmembers trained. Now we anticipated the arrival of May 14, 2004, so that we could start up the Missouri River on our travels to the far ocean.

The Second Leg of Four

May 14 to November 2, 2004

May 14, 2004, was a cold, dismal day. The weather was so bad that we loaded our boats under a bridge in Wood River in an attempt to stay dry. This weather was a sample of what we endured for the first thirty days of our trip up the Missouri River after leaving Camp Dubois. The 1804 group encountered the same problems as the journals were littered with troubling weather conditions at this junction of their journey.

Our departure from Camp Dubois was part of one of the National Council of the Lewis and Clark Bicentennial's fifteen signature events. Six of these events were scheduled for this leg of our trip, the most events for any one of the four legs. I was privileged to participate in eleven of these events.

Let's take a moment and look at all of these signature events because they were an integral part of our reenactment.

In chronological order they are:

- Bicentennial Inaugural: Jefferson's West, January 18, 2003, at Monticello, Charlottesville, Virginia. Unfortunately, this is one of the four events I missed. Some of our Discovery Expedition of St. Charles members did attend and had the privilege of firing a salute with their muskets and rifles from the roof of Monticello, signaling the beginning of the bicentennial event. They are very proud to have been part of the inaugural event, even though it was about seven degrees and extremely cold outside while waiting for the signal to fire a salute. They have a right to be proud.

- Falls of the Ohio, October 14–26, 2003, at Louisville, Kentucky, and Clarksville, Indiana. It was here that Captain Clark joined Captain Lewis, and the expedition became the famous Lewis and Clark Expedition. It was also here that while we were camped at Clarksville, a woman from Clarksville arrived at our camp each morning before breakfast with warm blueberry muffins. It is funny how you remember little things like that at such a monumental time in history. I wish I could remember her name because I would like to see her again and kiss her for her thoughtfulness. She exemplifies the spirit of the people we met during our travels across this grand and glorious country of ours.

- The Three Flags Ceremony, March 10–14, 2004, in St. Louis, Missouri. Some of us arrived on the white pirogue for the ceremony. There were approximately thirty-five members of the Discovery Expedition of St. Charles standing in formation during the ceremony in the shadow of the famous St. Louis Arch. This signature event commemorated the transfer of the Louisiana Territory from the possession of France to the United States. The third flag involved was that of Spain because at the time Spain was administrating the territory for France.

- Expedition's Departure: Camp River Dubois, May 13–16, 2004, at Illinois Lewis and Clark State Historical Site, Hartford, Illinois. I should now explain that there are two Camp Duboises. As mentioned before, the Camp Dubois in Wood River, Illinois, was built by C. J. Lanahan and used by the Discovery Expedition of St. Charles. The Camp River Dubois replica was built for and used by the Illinois Lewis and Clark State Historical Site, Hartford, Illinois. After leaving Wood River, we traveled a few miles downstream to the Hartford, Illinois site, where we were greeted by an estimated 6,000 people. While at Hartford, a prayer was said for our safe trip. We then crossed the Mississippi River and started up the Missouri River.

- St. Charles: Preparations Complete, the Expedition Faces West, May 14–23, 2004, at St. Charles, Missouri. Just like the original expedition, we arrived at St. Charles on May 16. Here we drilled, had daily parades, and made final preparations for the forthcoming journey. It rained, and rained, and rained; not really a pleasant stay in St. Charles. There were intervals of clear skies, but not very many.

- Heart of America: a Journey Fourth, July 3–4, 2004, at Kansas City, Missouri, Atchison, and Leavenworth, Kansas. A fine Fourth it was too, in Atchison, Kansas. While there, the skies opened up, giving us a torrential downpour with lightning. One lightening bolt hit a flag-pole in our vicinity and knocked the ball on top of the pole off while one of our tents was blown into the next county. Quite an exciting Fourth. The fireworks in Kansas City were canceled because of bad weather. The fireworks in Atchison were televised to Kansas City in lieu of their fire-works display. Atchison was lucky, in that their fireworks were able to be displayed between showers. All in all, a fine Fourth, and one to remember.

- First Tribal Council, July 31–August 3, 2004, at Fort Calhoun and Omaha, Nebraska. I missed this signature event because I was not on the river at the time. This signature event is dedicated to President Jefferson's wishes for the Corps of Discovery to establish relations with the American Indians. This was the corps' first contact with the Oto and Missouria tribes, which occurred at "Council Bluff."

- I was on the river a week before and a week after the Sergeant Floyd Burial Commemoration on August 20 in Sioux City, Iowa.

- Oceti Sakowin Experience: Remembering and Educating, August 27–September 26, 2004, at Oacoma/Chamberlain, South Dakota. Unfortunately, I was not on the river for this signature event either. This signature event is an effort to educate visitors to remember experiences prior to, during, and after Lewis and Clark visited the Oceti Sakowin (Seven Council Fires).

- Circle of Cultures: Time of Renewal and Exchange, October 22–31, 2004, at Bismarck, North Dakota. The University of Mary was an excellent choice for the presentations of the academically acclaimed guest lecturers. We camped at Kimball Bottom, which was a short distance from the university. The recently constructed earth lodges added immensely to the tone and visual aspects of this signature event.

- Explore! The Big Sky, June 1–July 4, 2005, at Fort Benton and Great Falls, Montana. I arrived at Great Falls just as this signature event was ending. But I was impressed by the Big Sky Country. Unfortunately, there are only three of the five Great Falls left, as described by Captain Lewis. Two of the falls are under water, covered by the water in the lakes created by the three dams. Only a trickle of the original water is now allowed to flow over the rocks. What a pity. After seeing the trail followed by the men of 1805 from the lower portage camp to the upper portage camp, I have a renewed admiration for their determination and grit in the face of almost impossible odds. I have said it before, and I will say it again. They were supermen.

- Destination: the Pacific, November 24–27, 2005, at Long Beach, Washington, to Cannon Beach, Oregon. Finally, as written in the journal, "Ocian in view! O! the joy." My sentiments exactly. These expressions, scribbled by Captain Clark, are two of the most famous expressions in American history. They convey a finality that can only be experienced by the men of the original expedition, and the men and women of the Discovery Expedition of St. Charles who have traveled in their footsteps and experienced some of their hardships. The camaraderie generated by the reenactors of today is of the same quality as the camaraderie generated 200 years ago. Now that the Pacific has been reached, there is so much to see and do in this area. Several things were mentioned in the journals, such as Dismal Nitch, Station Camp, whale bones, Cape Disappointment, the salt works, and finally Fort Clatsop. The metal tree and getting your feet wet wading in the Pacific Ocean are add-ons. We had one huge advantage over the men of 200 years ago, and that was cold beer.

- Among the Niimiipuu (The Nez Perce), June 14–17, 2006, at Lewiston, Idaho. The Lewis and Clark State College Campus was a perfect place to have this signature event. Auditoriums and classrooms were available for presentations and the outside campus area gave us an excellent place to pitch our tents and set up our exhibit stations for public viewing. The Nez Perce Indians and other tribes also took advantage of this area to exhibit and sell their handmade jewelry and other items. Finally, we were close enough to the college's computer labs that we could use their Internet connections.

- Clark On The Yellowstone, July 22–25, 2006, at Pompey's Pillar National Monument in Billings, Montana. Here is where the catamarans made me feel very comfortable in a dugout canoe. Up until this point we had single dugout canoes, and they were unstable as far as I am concerned, but the catamarans reestablished my faith in Captain Clark. Pompey's Pillar was an exciting signature event from the Indians on horseback parade to the reenactment of Captain Clark carving his name into sandstone on July 25. It was extremely hot, but no humidity; therefore, the heat was bearable.

- Reunion at the Home Of Sacagawea, August 17–20, 2006, at Mandan, Hidatsa, and Arikara Nations, New Town, North Dakota. The Indian Powwow at the Antelope Arbor was unbelievable. There were about 343 competitors all dancing in the sunlight during their warm up. The flash of color from the feathers, beads, and jingle bells is hard to put into words. It was phenomenal. Your mind's eye can picture the beauty of this event. It was very difficult to leave this encampment.

- Confluence with Destiny: the Return of Lewis and Clark, September 23–24, 2006, at the Greater St. Louis Metropolitan Area. I wish there were an expression like "Ocian in view! O! the joy!" to end our unbelievable journey, but alas, there is not. The original corps came home with much fanfare just as we did, but we had no lasting famous statement. Maybe I can make one up. "I am sorry that it is over." This is not true because the Lewis and Clark journey will never end for some of us. Long live Lewis and Clark.

This gives you an idea as to what we as reenactors experienced. The National Council of the Lewis and Clark Bicentennial should be commended for their planning of these signature events, but let's not forget the people who put these events into play. The list is too long to mention it now. I will give many of these organizations their true acknowledgment at the end of this book. Stay tuned if you worked to make this journey a success.

The following table is a list of our scheduled stops on our way to Fort Mandan, North Dakota. We have tried to track the original journey by camping at known campsites or as close to the original locations as possible.

Recorded 1804	Planned 2004	Missouri River Miles
May 14 Depart Wood River	May 14 Depart Camp Dubois	00
	May 14 Wilderness Camp	7.0
May 16 Arrive St Charles	May 15 Arrive St Charles MO	27
May 21 Depart St Charles	May 23 Dpt St Charles, MO	
May 23 Tavern Rock	May 23–24 Weldon Spring Access, MO	49
	May 24 Tavern Cave, MO	52
May 25 Lacherette	May 24–26 Washington, MO	68
	May 26–27 New Haven, MO	81.5
May 27 Mouth of Gasgonade River	May 27–28 Hermann, MO	97.5
	May 28 Chamois, MO	118
	May 29–Jun 1 Ike Skelton National Guard Training Center, MO	137
Jun 1 - 2 Mouth of Osage River	Jun 1–3 Jefferson City, MO	144
	Jun 3–4 Wilton, MO	161.9

	Jun 4–5 Lupus, MO	174
	Jun 5–6 Huntsdale, MO	180
Jun 7 Mouth of the Moniteau Creek	Jun 6–7 Rocheport, MO	186.4
	Jun 7–8 Boonville, MO	197
Jun 9 Arrow Rock	Jun 8–9 Arrow Rock	210.9
	Jun 9–11 Glasgow, MO Stump Island Recreation Park	225.7
Jun 13 Mouth of the Grand River	Jun 11–13 Brunswick, MO Mouth of the Grand River	250
	Jun 13–14 Miami, MO	262.8
	Jun 14–16 Wilderness Camp	270
Jun 17 Rope Walk Camp	Jun 16–17 Waverly, MO	294
	Jun 17–18 Lexington, MO	316.5
Jun 23 Fort Osage	Jun 18–24 Fort Osage, MO	337
	Jun 24–26 LaBenite Park, MO	352.5

Jun 26 - 29 Mouth of the Kansas River	Jun 26–29 Kansas City, KS Kaw Point	367.5
	Jun 29–Jul 1 Parkville, MO	377.9
	Jul 1–2 Leavenworth, KS	397.3
Jul 4 Independence Creek	Jul 2–5 Atchison, KS	423
	Jul 5–7 St Joseph, MO	444
	Jul 7–9 Wilderness Camp	462.6
Jul 12 Mouth of the Big Nemaha River	Jul 9–12 White Cloud (Little Tarkio)	488
	Jul 12–16 Wilderness Camp	519
Jul 16 Bald-pated Prairie (Loess Hills)	Jul 16–19 Brownville, NE	535.3
	Jul 19–22 Wilderness Camp	542
Jul 24 Camp White Catfish	Jul 22–25 Nebraska City, NE	562.3
	Jul 25–26 Plattsmouth, NE	592
Jul 26 Mouth of the Platte River	Jul 26–28 Bellvue, NE	601.3
	Jul 28–30 Omaha, NE	618.1

Aug 3 Meeting with Oto and Missouri Indians	Jul 30–Aug 6 Fort Calhoun, NE Fort Atkinson State Park	643
	Aug 6–7 Blair, NE	651
	Aug 7–9 Little Sioux River	669.1
	Aug 9–15 Decatur, NE	691.4
	Aug 15–16 Winnabago, Lake	708.8
	Aug 16–17 Wilderness Camp	721
AUG 18 Pvt Reed Captured	Aug 17–19 Dakota City, NE	725.5
Aug 20 Floyd's Burial	Aug 19–20 Sioux City, IA	731.5
	Aug 20–21 Ponca, NE	752
Aug 22 Gass Election	Aug 21–23 Elk Point, SD	779
	Aug 23–24 Vermillion, SD	795
Aug 25 Spirit Mound	Aug 24–30 Yankton, SD Gavins Point Dam (Portage)	811
Sep 4 Mouth of the Niobrara River	Sep 4–7 Springfield, SD	833

Sep 8 Prairie Dog Captured	Sep 7–9 Fort Randall, SD Fort Randall Dam (Portage)	880
	Sep 9–11 Gregory, SD Whetstone Bay Rec Area	901
	Sep 11–13 Snake Creek Area	921
	Sep 13–15 Plum Creek	942
Sep 16 - 17 Plum Creek	Sep 15–20 Chamberlain, SD	965
	Sep 20 Fort Thompson, SD Big Bend Dam (Portage)	987
	Sep 21–24 Joe Creek Area	1002
Sep 25 Mouth of the Bad River Confrontation with Teton Sioux	Sep 24–27 Fort Pierre, SD	1058
	Sep28–29 Oahe Dam–Portage	1072
	Sep 29–30 Spring Creek Resort, SD	1088.5
	Sep 30–Oct 1 Pike Haven, SD	1103.5
	Oct 1–2 Sutton Bay, SD	1136

	Oct 2–4 Forest City, SD	1153
	Oct 4–7 West Whitlock, SD	1153
	Oct 7–8 Swan Creek, SD	1174
Oct 8 Mouth of the Grand River	Oct 8–11 Mobridge, SD Indian Creek	1192
	Oct 11–12 Shaw Creek, SD	1218.5
Oct 13 Pvt Newman Punished	Oct 12–15 West Pollock, SD	1224
	Oct 15–16 Fort Yates, ND	1244.5
	Oct 16–18 Walker Bottom,ND	1257.5
	Oct 18–19 Hazelton, ND Fort Rice	1276.5
	Oct 19–20 Graner Park, ND	1296
Oct 20 On-A-Slant Indian Village	Oct 20–24Kimball Bottom,ND	1299.5
Oct 26 Met Mandan Chiefs	Oct 24–28 Fort Lincoln, ND	1311
	Oct 28–29 Eagle Park, ND	1318

	Oct 29–30 Steckel Boat Ramp	1338
	Oct 30–31 Cross Ranch State Park, ND	1356
	Oct 31–Nov 1 Washburn, ND	1363
	Nov 1–2 Knife River Indian Village, ND	
Nov 2 Fort Mandan Area	Nov 2–4 Fort Mandan, ND	

We had eighty-three scheduled encampments, and we made all eighty-three encampments. As we crossed the Mississippi River and entered the Missouri River, we were greeted by 100 people or so on the north bank of the Missouri River at Confluence State Park in Missouri.

On May 15, we arrived at St. Charles, Missouri, where we were welcomed by an estimated crowd of 10,000 people. We were humbled by this outpouring of cheers and applause. As we moved single file through the crowd from our boats to our campsite, we all had a feeling of pride and exhilaration. We received comments such as, "You look great," "Nice job," "Way to go," "Keep up the good work," "Welcome, I wish I were you," and on and on. How could you not feel anything but pride as your fellow citizens greeted you with these kinds of compliments? I am at a loss to truly express my feeling at that moment, but this feeling was to appear again and again as we moved through many, many crowds on our way to and from the Pacific Ocean.

Our nine days in St. Charles were full of visits by schoolchildren and other interested visitors. Each day we had a flag-raising formation, a pass in review parade, and a retreat formation. On May 17, Privates Hugh Hall and William Warner were court-martialed for coming in late one evening, as described in the journals. They were both found guilty and sentenced to twenty-five lashes. After the captains read the court-martial report, they said that these men did not deserve lashes and commuted that portion of the verdict pertaining to lashes. Many other events, found in the journals, were portrayed during our stay in St. Charles. This was a memorable nine days despite the almost constant rain.

On May 24, we put about ten men ashore to visit Tavern Cave because it was purported to contain an inscription with Sergeant Ordway's name and dated '04. I remained on the boat. The men climbed the bank and then disappeared into the thickets. They found railroad tracks and followed them to an area near the cave's entrance. The boats moved on ahead a short distance further. Several hours later, we fired the blunderbuss trying to let the land party know where we were. The original expedition did the same thing 200 years ago in an effort to contact men on shore. We had no response. During our travels through Missouri, the Missouri Conservation Department assigned one of their patrol boats to accompany us and to render any assistance that may be needed. This boat found our men several miles head of us and ferried them back to our boats. This little episode tells you how difficult it was for the original expedition to remain in contact when men were sent ashore. Men on shore were not unusual because of the hunting needed to maintain a food supply for the rest of the corps, and the exploring needed to be done to conform to President Jefferson's directives.

The next stop was at Washington, Missouri, where we were warmly welcomed and participated in a town parade and ceremonies in our honor. When members of the corps were dressed in their blue uniforms, shouldering their muskets, and in formation for a parade, they were very impressive. You must be photogenic to be a member of the Discovery Expedition of St. Charles because wherever you go, you are photographed.

After Washington, Missouri, we stopped at New Haven, Missouri. The good people of New Haven gave us the key to the city, which is a small key-shaped pin to be worn on a lapel or some other suitable attire. It was a very friendly gesture. New Haven claims John Colter as their native son. We participated in a dedication ceremony for Private Colter, which again honored him for his participation in the Lewis and Clark Expedition. The television and press coverage was quite extensive for a small community.

From May 29 to June 1, which was Memorial Day weekend, we camped at the Ike Skelton National Guard Training Center with 3,000 Boy Scouts, quite a show with this amount of interested scouts. Unfortunately, I put my bedroll on the ground without a tarp or camp cot. This allowed chiggers to feast on me. Now, chiggers are small mites that enter into the pores of your skin and die. They then become little red welts and itch like mosquito bites. With twenty or twenty-five of these welts, you become very uncomfortable. I was very uncomfortable. There is no mention of chiggers in the journals. I wonder if some of the comments about mosquitoes being very bothersome could have been chiggers bothering the members of the original Corps.

While our Corps was camped at Waverly, Missouri, on June 16, Seaman, our Newfoundland dog, died. Everyone was heartbroken because Seaman had become a loyal member of our expedition. He was only a year and a half old. His remains were sent to the University of Missouri's Veterinarian School for an autopsy, but the autopsy results were inconclusive as to a cause of death. Another Newfoundland dog was purchased, but we could not keep him in camp. He kept running away, so he was returned to the former owner. One of our members, Mike Dotson, brought his Newfoundland dog to camp when he was on the river and his Seaman worked out fine. We were very grateful to Mike for furnishing us with a very important piece of our period correctness.

Our next major stop was Kaw Point, Kansas City, Kansas. We were camped here from June 26–29. Kaw Point is a beautiful new riverfront park on the north bank of the Kansas River at its confluence with the Missouri River. The view from Kaw Point of the

Kansas City, Missouri, skyline is outstanding. Even darkness does not diminish this view as the lighted buildings of downtown Kansas City are just as picturesque as the buildings are during daylight.

Per the journals, on June 29, a major court-martial was conducted for Privates Hugh Hall and John Collins for drinking corps whiskey. Collins was the corps' guard on duty that night. Hall pled guilty and was sentenced to fifty lashes. Collins pled not guilty, was found guilty, and since he was the guard on duty, was then sentenced to one hundred lashes. They both received their lashes. All elements of the court-martial were reenacted before a large gathering of visitors, except the administering of lashes (thank goodness because I portrayed Private Hall during the re-enactment).

We spent July 1–2 camped in the parks and recreation area of Leavenworth, Kansas. This encampment brought back fond memories because during my army career I had spent some time at Fort Leavenworth attending the Army Command and General Staff College. Like most other things, Fort Leavenworth has and has not changed over the years.

July 4 was spent at Atchison, Kansas. As a matter of fact, we were camped in Atchison from July 2–5. This was a national signature event and attended by some 60,000 people during the weekend. Naturally, we had a parade through town on the Fourth. We were joined by many other military and non-military units. Of course, we were the finest unit in the parade and received an abnormal amount of cheers and applause as we passed through town. Then many speeches were made while we stood in ranks at Atchison's riverside park. It was quite a festive weekend, climaxed by a super fireworks presentation between showers. As did the original Corps, we fired our bow pieces in celebration of the Fourth. When we left Atchison, we passed Independence Creek (also known as Fourth of July Creek) and again fired a salute.

The next stop was St. Joseph, Missouri from July 5–7. It was here that Les Nelson of St. Joseph, Missouri, approached me. I was leaving the boat, and he asked me if I wanted to see the boats from his airplane. I couldn't believe what he was offering, but quickly said, "Yes." He took me to a local airport, and we were quickly airborne. The bird's eye view from aloft was fascinating. He pointed out a dry ox bow and the park at Atchison where we had been camped over the Fourth of July weekend. I took pictures of our boats tied up at St. Joseph. It was quite a unique perspective compared with the views the men had in 1804. This airplane excursion reiterates that we do live in the twenty-first century.

We were camped at Decatur, Nebraska from July 9–15. Two notable things happened while we were camped here. The first was the ungodly amount of corn given to us by a local vendor. Decatur went all out to welcome us, including a three-day festival at their riverfront park where we were camped. There were many vendors at this festival selling everything from souvenirs to food. One vendor was selling steamed corn on the cob. Since Nebraska is corn country and July is the season for corn, he had a truckload of fresh corn at his tent. After the festival was over, he had crates and crates of unsold corn. He then proceeded to donate all of the left over corn to the Corps.

Now, we men in the Corps don't mind being fed by the locals after all, this is what happened 200 years ago, but we really don't need a donation of 200 pounds of fresh corn. We were already sick and tired of parched corn. But the powers to be in our organization were very happy to accept this donation because it meant that they did not have to buy some fresh vegetable groceries as a result of this donation; a monetary savings which made them starry-eyed.

As we stowed the corn on our boats, I believe the boats listed to starboard about seventy degrees until we balanced the cargo. Then, you guessed it—we had corn at all of our meals for days, and days, and days. We had corn in our salads, in our pancakes, in our sandwiches, in our desserts, and finally in our dreams. I believe we eventually shot some of the corn out of our bow guns as a salute, unbeknownst to our cadre and cooks. Who said that this trip was serious business and you couldn't have a few laughs while on the river?

The second notable event while in Decatur was meeting Butch Bouvier, who lives in Onawa, Iowa. As a matter of fact, I believe he lives on or at least very near Blue Lake. Bouvier makes keelboats. At the time Rex Becker and I spoke with him, he had made some eight or ten keelboats, mostly for museums. During our visit, Bouvier was very hospitable and showed us around his boatyard. He had a couple of boats under construction. This was a very informative side trip for both Rex and I.

Then came Floyd's burial. Sergeant Floyd was the only member of the expedition to die during the journey. From the journal entries about treating a sick Sergeant Floyd, modern medical science has concluded that Sergeant Floyd probably died of appendicitis. The symptoms mentioned in the journals concur with today's knowledge of the sickness. Appendicitis was unknown to the medical profession of 1804. Consequently, his death was apparently a natural death. The fact that only one man died during this journey is amazing, especially when you look at the hardships and dangers the men of the expedition faced during their three-year journey. Not only is it amazing, it is miraculous.

We camped on the grounds of the new interpretive center in Sioux City, Iowa, on August 19–20. Here we met the Sergeant Floyd Brigade of the Lewis and Clark Trail Heritage Foundation. The brigade had about nine or ten men for the reenactment of Floyd's burial. They do this reenactment every year. We reinforced their organization with about twenty of our men for this year's reenactment. Floyd's Monument sits high on a hill overlooking the Missouri River, a very beautiful and commanding view. The burial reenactment took place at the bottom of the hill in a field a couple hundred yards from a tree line. We assembled at his monument on top of the hill, and then proceeded to march downhill through a tree-covered slope for about 200 yards. Then crossing a field for another hundred yards or so, finally arriving at the gravesite. Words were spoken by the two captains, a sergeant, and several of his fellow soldiers. Then a musket salute was fired, ending the burial commemoration, a very solemn and militarily conducted occasion.

A manikin of Sergeant Floyd's remains was carried by four men on a boat's hatch cover. This burial reenactment was performed twice on August 20. Once at one p.m. with about 2,000 spectators and again at about four p.m. with a couple of hundred spectators, which surprised me because I thought that the later burial would attract more interested people. There was very extensive TV coverage because of our involvement in the reenactment.

While camped at Elk Point, South Dakota, on August 21–23, some electioneering could be heard around our campfire. It seems that some of our men were soliciting votes to be the new sergeant. One man promised no kitchen police for any man who would vote for him. Another man was heard promising an extra whiskey ration for anyone who voted for him. Patrick Gass was elected by his peers and then appointed a sergeant by Captain Lewis to replace Sergeant Floyd on August 25. While in Elk Point, we were invited to make our own sundaes at Edgar's. Edgar's is a 1950s soda fountain. What a hoot. Just picture twenty or so grown men behind a soda fountain concocting their own sundaes. We had many, many pleasant experiences on this journey.

The next stop was Vermillion, South Dakota, on August 23–24 and a trip to Spirit Mound. In 1804, the captains were told by the Indians that little devils, or demons, eighteen inches tall, inhabited the mound, and it was not safe to go near the mound. The captains found no little men. Nor did we, but we did find a commanding view of the surrounding area when we reached the top. The title, Plains Country, is an excellent choice for this area because from this vantage point, the surrounding countryside is flat, flat, flat. There are a few trees in gullies or swales, but on the whole, there is just flat grassland and farmland for as far as you can see. This is a view of our vast country that joins the mix to make our country one of a kind. This stop was another milestone in our quest to reach the Pacific Ocean.

We finally reached Yankton, South Dakota, and the Gavin's Point Dam on August 25. Gavin's Point Dam does not have a lock. Consequently, after over 800 miles of free-flowing water on the Missouri River, we had to portage around the dam. We do have trailers for all three boats, and the portage was made without incident. The South Dakota National Guard did lend an assist. They provided heavy-duty trucks to pull our trailered boats. We have equipment that can pull our trailered boats, but their heavy-duty equipment made life a little easier.

It was at this point that I went home till October 12. Upon my return, I stayed on the river till the corps reached Fort Mandan, North Dakota, on November 2. My drive to Philadelphia, Pennsylvania, was a two-night trip. That means a round trip from Philadelphia took six days on the road to spend two weeks on the river. This traveling time and distance does not make short river trips worth the effort, especially since the Corps was traveling farther and farther west. Consequently, in 2005 and 2006, I was on the river for twelve of the fourteen months that the Discovery Expedition of St. Charles was on the river.

I rejoined the Corps on October 12 at West Pollock, South Dakota. On October 13, we reenacted the court-martial of Private John Newman for making "mutinous expressions" in the Pollock High School gymnasium. He was found guilty, sentenced to seventy-five lashes, and banished from the Corps. Private Newman stayed with the Corps until the keelboat was returned to St. Louis from Fort Mandan in the spring of '05. He was on board the keelboat at that time. The hundred or so spectators in the gymnasium were explained to, in detail, the reasons for the court-martials during the expedition. This was the last encampment in South Dakota.

We subsequently camped at Fort Yates, Walker Bottom, Fort Rice, Graner Park, and Kimball Bottom, all in North Dakota.

Our stay at Kimball Bottom was from October 20–24. During

this period, we were privileged to take part in the Circle of Cultures National Signature Event at the University of Mary in Bismark, North Dakota. Some of the notable speakers were James Ronda, Clay Jenkinson, Tom Theissen, Dayton Duncan, Ray Wood, Amy Mossett, and many more. The recently constructed earth lodges on the campus were very impressive and added an aesthetic value to the signature event. Our presence in uniform also added flavor to the event. While in the Bismarck area, the Elks Club 1199 hosted us on several evenings to watch football games on television. After all, none of us forgot about Monday night football.

Our next encampment was Fort Lincoln, North Dakota, from October 24–28. While at the fort, we visited the On-a-Slant Indian Village. The name comes from the ground on which the village was built. There were some seventy-five earth lodges there at the village. The village was active from about 1630 to 1750. The earth lodges had been abandoned for some time when Lewis and Clark visited the village in 1804. It was also explained how the Fort played a part in the life of Colonel George Armstrong Custer. He was fort commander at Fort Lincoln and left Fort Lincoln in 1876 with the 7th Calvary. They followed the Sioux Indians into the Little Bighorn Valley.

We camped at the Cross Ranch State Park from October 30–31. The rangers at the park were very accommodating and made our stay at the park comfortable.

We arrived at Fort Mandan on November 2 with much fanfare. The state of North Dakota has built a beautiful interpretive center in Washburn and a replica of Fort Mandan a couple of miles away. It is believed that the original site of Fort Mandan is now under water. We camped in the field outside of the fort. David Borlaug, director of the site, and his staff were very accommodating. The crowd was quite large and anxious to greet us because this was the last stop in our journey in 2004. Once again, that feeling of accomplishment came back to me as I walked through this vast welcoming crowd. It had been a long six months' journey on the river. The boats are tired and so are the men. We found a local watering hole, the Captain's Cabin, and as usual, they welcomed us with open arms. As a matter of fact, we were asked to sign a rather large blimp hanging from the ceiling. About thirty of us signed our names on the blimp. This was almost as good as a ceiling tile.

We loaded the boats on their trailers, packed all of our gear into our vehicles, said our good-byes, and headed for home on November 4th.

2004 was a very pleasant and fruitful year for the Discovery Expedition of St. Charles. We accomplished all that we intended to accomplish, and looked forward to April 7, 2005.

The Third Leg of Four

April 7 to November 26, 2005

Our crew started arriving at Fort Mandan on April 4, 2005. During the next three days, our men were coming in from all parts of the country and the red and white pirogues arrived from St. Charles, Missouri. It took me three days to drive from Philadelphia, Pennsylvania, to Fort Mandan, North Dakota. Consequently, a two-week stay on the river was now out of the question. During this leg of our journey, I was on the river for the first thirty days, went home for sixty days, and then returned to the river and stayed on the trail for the next five months.

The stay at Fort Mandan was very productive because we spoke with several hundred schoolchildren during this period. I also met Pennsylvania State Representative Lynn Herman at this time. A departure ceremony was held at the fort on the seventh. We marched from the fort to the boats amid about 700 interested spectators, boarded the boats, and were off to the Pacific Ocean at about three p.m. in the two pirogues. The weather was cool and no rain. What a blessing.

It must be remembered that from Fort Mandan, North Dakota,

to Lemhi Pass, Idaho, the original Corps did not see another human being for four months or about 1,000 miles plus. But I am sure that many pairs of eyes watched them as they passed on their journey.

We had the British Broadcasting Company (BBC) crew with us for the first thirty days of this leg. They were Jim Price and Matt Share. Both of these men were filming our daily activities for a BBC special as part of their PBS series. Along with filming daily routines, they took hours and hours of interviews. I have not seen or heard about the fruits of their labors.

During this leg of our journey, we had seventy-six scheduled encampments. Here is a list of these encampments.

Recorded 1805	Recorded 2005
	Apr 4–7 Ft Mandan, ND
Apr 7 Left Fort Mandan. Keelboat sent back to St Louis.	Apr 7 Pirogues Depart Ft Mandan to Knife River Indian Village, Stanton, ND
	Apr 8–10 Knife River Indian Village
	Apr 11–12 Indian Hills Resort, Garrison, ND
	Apr 13–14 Wilderness Camp
	Apr 15–17 New Town, ND
	Apr 18 Wilderness Camp
	Apr 19–21 Herman Park, Williston, ND
	Apr 22 Wilderness Camp
	Apr 23–25 Ft Buford, ND and the Confluence of the Yellowstone and Missouri Rivers

	Apr 26 Wilderness Camp
	Apr 27 Culbertson, MT
	Apr 28 Brockton, MT
	Apr 29 Sprole, MT
	Apr 30 Poplar, MT
	May 1–4 Wolf Point, MT
May 8 At the Milk River.	May 5–10 Fort Peck Dam, MT
May 11 Lewis would rather fight two Indians than one bear.	May 11–17 Jordan, MT
May 20 At the Muscleshell River	May 18–24 Kipp State Park
	May 25–31 Upper Missouri Breaks National Monument
	Jun 1 Wilderness Camp
Jun 3 At the Marias River.	Jun 2–Jul 9 Great Falls, MT (Explore the Big Sky National Signature Event)
	Jul 10–11 Broadwater Bay, Great Falls, MT
	Jul 12 Wilderness Camp
	Jul 13 Big Bend Public Fishing Access Camp
	Jul 14 Ulm, MT
	Jul 15 Cascade, MT
	Jul 16–17 Pelican Point Fishing Access Camp, MT
	Jul 18 Holter Dam Campground, MT

Jul 19 Lewis calls the view "gates of the rocky mountains".	Jul 19 Travel Through Gates of the Mountains, MT
	Jul 20 Devil's Elbow Campground, MT
	Jul 21 Hellsgate Campground Canyon Ferry Lake
	Jul 22 White Earth Campground
Jul 25 At the Three Forks.	Jul 23–25 Three Forks, MT (Headwaters of the Missouri River)
	Jul 26–27 Townsend, MT
Jul 28 The Captains name the three river Jefferson River, Madison River and Gallatin River.	Jul 28 Three Forks, MT
	Jul 29–31 Lewis and Clark Caverns State Park, MT
	Aug 1 Whitehall, MT
	Aug 2–4 Twin Bridges, MT
	Aug 5–9 Dillon, MT
	Aug 10–14 Barrett, MT
Aug 13 Lewis meets the Shoshone Indians	Aug 12 Commemorative Ceremony of Crossing Lemhi Pass
	Aug 15 Grant, MT
	Aug 16 James Ranch, MT
Aug 17 Sacajewea recognizes her brother Cameahwait.	Aug 17 Lemhi Pass
Aug 21 At the Lewis River.	Aug 18–28 Salmon, ID

	Aug 29–31 Tower Rock, ID
	Sep 1–3 Lost Trail Hot Springs, MT
	Sep 4–6 Darby, MT
Sep 9 At Traveler's Rest	Sep 7–10 Traveler's Rest, Lolo, MT
	Sep 11–12 Lolo Hot Springs, MT
	Sep 13–14 Lolo Summit, MT
	Sep 15–19 Lolo Trail, ID
Sep 20 Find Nez Perce Indians.	Sep 20–25 Weippe, ID
Sep 26 Setup Canoe Camp and make dugouts.	Sep 26–Oct 7 Canoe Camp, Orofino, ID
	Oct 8–10 Clarkston, WA
	Oct 11 Boyer Park, Almota, WA
	Oct 12 Central Ferry State Park, WA
	Oct 13 Lyons Ferry, WA
Oct 17 At the Columbia River	Oct 14–17 Sacajewea State Park, Pasco, WA
	Oct 18–19 Irrigon, OR
	Oct 20 Roosevelt Recreation Area, WA
Oct 22 Portaged Celilo Falls.	Oct 21–23 Maryhill State Park, WA
Oct 26 At the Rock Fort	Oct 24–27 Crates Point, Gorge Interpretive Center, Rock Fort, The Dalles, OR

	Oct 28 Viento State Park, Hood River, OR
	Oct 29–31 Cascade Locks, OR
	Nov 1 Rooster Rock State Park, OR
	Nov 2 Capt Wm Clark Park, Washougal, WA
	Nov 3 Frenchman's Bar, Vancouver, WA
	Nov 4 Kalama, WA
	Nov 5 County Line Park, Cathlamet, WA
	Nov 6 Vista Park, Skamokawa, WA
	Nov 7 Knappton Cove Quarantine Station, WA
Nov 10 - 14 Stuck on Dismal Nitch.	Nov 8–26 Chinook City Park, Chinook, WA
Nov 16 In plain view of the Pacific Ocean.	
Nov 24 Famous vote.	
Dec 8 Start Building Fort Clatsop.	

Our first stop was at the Knife River Indian Village. In 1805, there were about 120 earth lodges in this village with a population of approximately 3–5,000 people. We were privileged to be invited to view artifacts that were not normally on public display but stored in the site's archives. The curator described the cleaning, labeling, authenticating, and other preparations for preservation—a very informative presentation. We learned so much on this trip that my head hurts. Our actual campsite was in Stanton, Montana. The good people of Stanton fed us a warm breakfast on April 8, and buffet dinners the 8–9. We were very appreciative of this hospitality.

On April 11, we proceeded on to the Indian Hills Resort near Garrison, North Dakota. This may have been a water resort several years ago, but today it is a dry, parched area where the boat ramps no longer reach the water. This is the result of a seven-year drought in the area. In speaking with the owner of the resort, he stated that the resort was private property, and we had his permission to shoot a deer while we were on his property. This offer was immediately accepted by us. Questions of the state game laws regarding hunting on private property were immediately brought up, but apparently, the owner had us covered because we sent two hunting parties out in opposite directions. There were two or three men in each party with their flintlock muskets or rifles. No deer were shot, but one turkey was shot.

The April 13 and 14 encampment was at a wilderness camp on the banks of Lake Sakakawea on the Fort Berthold Indian Reservation. We were very close to the small town of White Shield, and we were invited to make a presentation at the local school. Since the school did not have a bus for the students to visit us, we accepted their invitation. We set up four stations, one in each of the four corners of the school's gymnasium. The stations were clothing, firearms/furs, artifacts, and medical procedures. The students spent a half an hour at each station. At the end of our presentation, we received a loud round of applause. As we exited the school, a teacher told us that these kids never applaud following a class presentation, and that their applause today was very unusual. This meant that we reached them with something of interest. Of course, this made our day, since one of our primary mission mandates is the education of schoolchildren.

The next stop was New Town, North Dakota, on April 15. New Town is also on the Fort Berthold Reservation and the administrative center for the Three Affiliated Tribes. The tribes are the Mandan, Hidatsa, and Arikara. Upon arrival at New Town, we were greeted by tribal members Scott Eagle and Dominick Sillitti. They invited us to participate in a town parade. We gladly accepted. The tribes offered one of their members, Jessica Grinnell, to portray Sacagawea. We again gladly accepted her and her small son, who portrayed Jean-Baptiste Charbonneau, also known as Pomp.

Following the parade, we asked to use the center's computers for an e-mail check. My brother had sent me an e-mail stating our mother had passed away the night before from renal failure. She was ninety-five years old and her death was not unexpected. Northwest Airline had a bereavement fare for about 50 percent of the cost of a regular ticket. I flew from Minot, North Dakota, to Minneapolis, to Philadelphia for the funeral, returning to the Corps a week later.

From April 23 to 25, we were camped on the banks of the Missouri River in view of the confluence of the Yellowstone River on the grounds of the Missouri-Yellowstone Confluence Interpretive Center. This center has a new beautiful building operated by the historical society of North Dakota. The remaining foundations for Fort Buford are located nearby. A visit to the Fort Buford cemetery is an eye opener. Reading the headstones gives you insight into how difficult life was on this outpost over 100 years ago. A short distance away is Fort Union, a fur trading post established in 1828. This date is only about twenty years after Lewis and Clark went through this area. Fort Union has been meticulously restored and is immaculately maintained. One interesting note about Fort Union is that half of its parking lot is in North Dakota and the other half is in Montana. This gives you a pretty good idea of its location.

On April 28, we were moving from a wilderness camp to Culbertson, Montana, on a windy, twenty-five-degree day. The trip was bone chilling. I can handle a twenty-degree day if there is no wind, but with a twenty-mile-per-hour wind, I turn into an icicle. As a matter of fact, we all bundled up and hunkered down, unless you were on the tiller. That was the hardest part of the trip—standing up in the wind and handling the tiller. All in all, this is another example of what the 1805 expedition experienced on their travels, and they did not have the gear and Under Armour underwear we had.

The Discovery Expedition of Saint Charles has a Web site. During our journey different men posted entries on this Web site in order to keep the men, who were not on the river, informed of our progress. The following entries were posted on the Web site by Private Hall.

Thursday, April 28, 2005
(Private Hugh Hall, Ed Scholl)

Reveille at 0700; the weather is overcast and dismal. The temperature was twenty-six degrees with snow showers in the morning. Breakfast consisted of scrambled eggs with bacon bits and pancakes that had walnut pieces mixed into the batter.

Two men are sick. Sergeant Pryor has a bad left leg. Private Shannon has a virus. Shannon was taken to the hospital and remains there. We are camped on the bank of the Missouri River about three miles from Culbertson, Montana. The hills on the north side of the river are fairly high, maybe 100 feet or so. South side of river is flat for maybe three miles, and then the hills rise just like the hills on the north side. This area is like a wide valley or flood plain, cut eons ago by the river.

Very cold and windy today; the high was around forty degrees. Eight men went to the Culbertson Elementary School. Uniforms, weapons, boats, medicine, and artifacts were the five stations that the children rotated through. There were approximately 120 children in attendance, and the presentation by the men was well received. Visited the Culbertson Museum, many, many artifacts and historical items on display. The people of Culbertson, Montana had a barbeque for the crew at 1730 hours. Well received by the crew. A dozen or so Boy Scouts were pictured with the crew and sought autographs.

Brockton, Montana, was our next stop on April 29, after spending nine cold hours on the river. Here we camped on the riverbank and cooked over an open fire. During the dinner preparation, we were visited by a man and a woman who worked in a nearby grain elevator. I think they felt sorry for us because of the cold weather, cooking outdoors, and sleeping on the boats. They invited us to breakfast in the grain elevator the next morning. The warm food and warm building were a blessing the next morning. I don't know how they did it, but the entire crew in the grain elevator pulled together and offered scrambled eggs, pancakes, bacon, sausage, toast, coffee, and Danish, along with syrup, butter, and other necessary condiments for the fifteen or so of us.

It was unbelievable how well people treated us as we crossed the country. We tried to reciprocate by telling them about our travels and adventures. When we sit down and speak with someone one-on-one, they become truly interested in our adventures. This was what happened in the Brockton grain elevator. All of the employees were completely attentive as we told them about our journey. I wish I could have done more for those wonderful people who have helped us cross this beautiful country of ours, but I have learned that a little thank you can go a long way in our society. So I thank you, Brockton grain elevator employees, for your thoughtfulness and hospitality.

Here it was May 1, and a four-night stay at Wolf Point, Montana. A lot warmer that day. We pulled the boats out of the water because of low water upstream. The Montana National Guard allocated assets to help us. Once again, the guard's heavy equipment made our job easier. The boats were quickly trailered and ready for movement to Fort Peck Lake, which was behind Fort Peck Dam. The local Lion's Club sponsored a fundraising barbecue for us. They expected about 150 people, and 300 people showed up. They ran out of food, had to resupply from town, and worked well into the afternoon. I heard that they generated about $600 for us. We thanked them for their efforts and support. On May 3, we were honored to have had U.S. Senator Conrad Burns visit our camp and welcome us to Montana. He was very supportive of our endeavors and thankful for our efforts. This kind of support was always welcomed in our camps.

May 5 found us at Fort Peck for five nights. Bob Strand visited us in the afternoon and stayed for four hours with his guitar, entertaining us with bluegrass and country western songs and music. The next day, he brought his four-piece band to our camp for a rehearsal for a gig they had that night at the Nashua Town Hall. They played during the afternoon and then went to Nashua. Nashua is a small community very close to Fort Peck. We followed them that evening and had a very entertaining evening.

Here it was July 10, and I was back on the river. We were camped at Broadwater Bay in Great Falls, Montana. The pirogues were no longer with the expedition. In 1805, they were cached below the Great Falls. We were now in dugout canoes. The two cottonwood dugouts had been furnished to us by the Missouri Conservation Department. We were now paddling dugouts six to ten hours per day. Three to six men were in a dugout, depending on the number of men we had on the river. After several hours of paddling, the routine becomes very monotonous. This drudgery continued as long as we were in dugouts. It was compounded by a blazing hot sun in July and August. Sunburn and dehydration were ever-present dangers when on the river for hours and hours. The boat captains had the prerogative to pull onto the riverbank for a pit stop or to eat lunch, but there were times when time was of the essence, and stops were kept to a minimum. One man eating lunch while the other men kept paddling was not infrequent.

Sitting in a dugout for hours on end had a tendency to cramp leg muscles. The opposite happens when you paddled for hours. Your back and arm muscles ache. Of course, after a month of this activity you do toughen up, but never completely. Moving a dugout upstream was exhausting. I couldn't wait till we were going downstream. But that didn't happen for another thousand miles. We had another problem the 1805–1806 expedition did not face. That is trailering the dugouts. Our dugouts weigh in excess of 2,000 pounds each.

Consequently, it was all but impossible to carry the dugouts. We had to find boat ramps to launch and to recover our dugouts because of all the dams on the rivers which required portaging. The original expedition had to portage, but their dugouts must have been much lighter than ours because I cannot see how these men could have carried a one-ton dugout any appreciable distance. If they did, they were truly supermen. Another consideration is that they did not portage as many times as we did. Their progress was not impeded by dams.

————

When Captain Lewis first saw the Great Falls, he was impressed. There were five falls. Today there are four falls, and three have a dam built above them. There is just a trickle of water coming over the falls today. The falls are the Great Falls and Ryan Dam, Crooked Falls, Rainbow Falls and Dam, and Black Eagle Falls and Dam. Colter Falls is submerged beneath the water behind Rainbow Falls Dam. The 1805 portage around these falls took approximately thirty days and covered eighteen miles. What a bear. The men made makeshift wheels to transport the dugouts around the falls. Upon failure to float the iron boat, for lack of a sealant, the men made two additional cottonwood dugout canoes and then proceeded on July 15. We were lucky because our dugouts had a trailer.

Clothing was another problem at about this time. The men's military cloth clothing was wearing out. Since there was no military resupply source or a Walmart in the area, the men had to resort to another source which was leather. When they shot an animal, they ate the meat and used the hides for clothing. Deer hides were better for clothing than elk or buffalo hides because they were more supple and lighter in weight. But elk hides were preferred for moccasins. In order to be historically or period correct, we were starting to wear leather clothing.

Many of our men made their own shirts and pants from tanned

hides purchased locally or through mail order. Much of our down-time was used for making or repairing leather clothing. I made leg-gings from hides I purchased through the Discovery Expedition of St. Charles' source, but I had a shirt made by a man in Nebraska and a pair of pants and a pair of moccasins made by a leather crafter in Klickitat, Washington.

Our footwear for cordelling, which is pulling the dugouts with ropes, was a problem. While cordelling the canoes, we were walking in mud, on sand, or on rocks. Walking on sand was no problem. It gave us a nice, firm, flat surface to walk on. Rocks were a problem if they were boulder size; otherwise walking on pebbles was not a prob-lem either. The major problem was mud. As you walked in mud, you would sink ankle deep. Then, as you lifted your foot to take another step, the mud would suck off your footwear. It was nigh impossible to keep moccasins on your feet while cordelling through mud. Some of our men went barefooted, but they risked the possibility of injury or serious cuts. Since moccasins were expensive and difficult to recover once they were stuck in the mud, we resorted to water shoes purchased from local outlets. A size smaller than normal was preferred because it created a better bond than a loose-fitting shoe. I always carried a pair of moccasins in my haversack, which was also known as a "possible bag," when paddling so that I could change shoes when necessary to maintain an appearance of period correctness.

We were on our way to Big Bend Public Fishing Access Camp on July 13. This was a seven-mile paddle. We cordelled about three miles. Cordelling was preferred that day because it was easier than paddling, and it was nice to be in the water on a hot ninety-degree day.

On July 14, we had a pleasant surprise at Ulm, Montana. As our dugouts paddled into Ulm, the volunteer fire department gave us an arch of water to paddle under. They had set up a fire hose on the bank of the river and sent an arch of water towering into the sky as a welcoming gesture. It was little things like this that made our journey so memorable.

A seventeen-mile paddle was on the agenda for July 19 as we went through the Gates of the Mountains, so named because of the steep cliffs and narrow portal for the river. It is truly an impressive sight to see this opening in the mountains and then to travel between the perpendicular walls. What an awesome experience! Many boaters use this area for recreational activities. It was not too bad when the boats slowed down to pass a dugout canoe, but problems occurred when the boaters did not slow down. Our dugouts have a low side-board distance between the water and the gunnel. We would take on water from a very small wave or wake. What compounded the problem were the walls of this narrow passage. Wakes reflected off the walls and reinforced other wakes, which caused turbulence in the narrows and consequently an unhealthy situation for dugout canoes. The 1805 expedition did not enjoy this modern-day luxury of seeing people in the Gates of the Mountains. They passed through this area unobstructed by boaters.

The National Park Service invited us to a concert at a picnic area within the gates. It was attended by about seventy people who all came on boats because there was no other way to get to the picnic area. We added color to the event because we were dressed in our blue uniforms. The music was excellent and included songs about Lewis and Clark, which made us feel right at home.

While we were in the Helena, Montana area, we were invited to a cookout at the home of George Donnelly and his wife, Virginia. George is a retired colonel from the Montana National Guard and was an excellent liaison for our Corps as we crossed Montana. The buffalo burgers and hospitality at their cookout led to a full evening of camaraderie. On our three-year journey, we were so lucky to have had our fellow Americans treat us to nothing but the best. We had our share of hardships, but these hardships were far outweighed by the generosity of people like the Donnellys.

On July 20, we camped at the Devil's Elbow Campground and participated in the dedication of a kiosk for the Two Camps Vista, in memory of Clete Daily. This vista is on a promontory. If you look downriver, you can see the location of one of the campsites of the 1805 expedition, and if you look upriver, you can see the location of the next campsite of the 1805 expedition, an unusual view. Our men in their dress blue uniforms made for a very colorful and military-orientated dedication. All went well. The geological terrain was now far different from that of South Dakota and the other plains states. We were looking at rugged outcroppings of rocks and the foothills of the Rocky Mountains.

The next day, July 21, we moved to Helsgate Campground on the Canyon Ferry Lake. Last night and this night were two of the worst nights of my life. The mosquitoes were horrendous. We did have modern mosquito spray and lotion repellants, which I am sure helped, but were not 100 percent effective. I can now appreciate what the men meant when they stated that the mosquitoes were bothersome.

We camped from July 23 to 25 at the Missouri Headwaters State Park in Three Forks, Montana. It is here that three rivers come together and form the Missouri River. Consequently, Captain Lewis stated that this was the headwaters of the mighty Missouri River. He and Captain Clark proceeded to name the three rivers Jefferson's River (in honor of President Jefferson), Madison's River (in honor of James Madison, the then Secretary of State), and Gallatin's River (in honor of Albert Gallatin the Secretary of the Treasury). Overlooking our campsite was Lewis' Rock, a huge 300-foot-high, white precipice. This rock formation has a commanding view of the countryside. One could see for miles and enjoy the thought that they were standing in Lewis' footprints. The juncture of the Jefferson and Gallatin Rivers was clearly visible. The junction of the Jefferson and Madison Rivers was a little difficult to discern. The view was awe-some as you looked at the rolling hills, tree-filled ravines, flowing rivers, beautiful blue sky, and mountains on the horizon.

On July 23, the community of Three Forks hosted us for din-ner. We reciprocated by making a Lewis and Clark presentation to about 300 people who came to our campsite for a visit and to hear the publicized presentation. The presentation was well received and concluded with the corps singing their signature songs consisting of "Shenandoah" and "Kentucky Women."

I had a pleasant surprise on July 24, when my daughter, Julie, stopped by with her husband and my two grandsons. They were on their way home to Seattle, Washington, after attending a wedding in Livingston, Montana. Naturally, the boys, ages eight and six, wanted to go for a ride in the dugouts and sleep in the tents. No luck on either account.

On July 25, we were all surprised and honored with an unexpected visit by Dr. Gary Moulton, the world-renowned expert on the Lewis and Clark journals. He was accompanying a group on a tour bus that was following the Lewis and Clark trail. Dr Moulton was very friendly and spoke favorably about the efforts of our expedition. Later that day, Clay Jenkinson, another Lewis and Clark aficionado, stopped by unannounced and favored us with his company for a short time. He too was with a bus tour.

Our Three Forks encampment was very productive for me. All of these visits broke the routine of normal camp life. That is reveille at 0700 hours, breakfast at 0730 hours, formation and flag raising at 0800 hours, and then paddling the boats for six to ten hours. Upon leaving Three Forks, we followed the Jefferson River to Twin Bridges, where the Jefferson River changes names to its original name, the Beaverhead River. The Beaverhead River was then followed till it was too shallow for the dugouts. This occurs at Camp Fortunate, which is now underwater in the Clark Canyon Dam Lake. The 1805 expedition stashed their canoes here and retrieved them on their return trip in 1806.

Next encampment was Townsend, Montana on July 26–27. On July 26, the local rotary club hosted a pig roast for us, which was an outstanding meal. Then on July 27, we were hosted by Len and Linda Reeves for an elk burger dinner, another outstanding meal. We were very fortunate to have all of these and many, many other hospitable and friendly people treat us with such kindness. We can't say thank you enough. While we were in Townsend, we visited the Crimson Bluffs that were so aptly described in the journals. They are truly crimson and worth a visit when you are in the neighborhood. They are best seen from the river because they stand about twenty to thirty feet high and are perpendicular to the river. The red or crimson rock stands out dramatically from the other rock formations in the area, so much so that it is worthy of a notation in the Lewis journal.

The Lewis and Clark Caverns State Park was our encampment for July 29–31. The caverns were never seen by the members of the expedition in 1805 or 1806, but they were subsequently discovered in 1882 and commercialized for public use. They are very interesting to visit. It takes about two hours to tour the caverns. While we were there, we were visited by members of the Blackfeet Tribe from the Two Medicine River area. They were led by Curly Bear Wagner and another elder of the tribe. Drummers accompanied them and played for a good portion of the afternoon. They ended their drumming performance with an honor song in our honor. We gifted each drummer and the elders with our crew medals. These social events with our Indian brothers allowed us to understand their plights and concerns. We, as a reenactment organization, cannot solve the problems, but we can certainly feel empathy for their problems.

August 2–4 were the dates of our encampment at Twin Bridges, Montana. This is also where the Jefferson River changes names to the Beaverhead River. I had another surprise as my youngest daughter, Kate, stops in for a visit with her husband. They were moving to the West Coast from New York City, and they were on their way to Spokane, Washington. This was another most welcome family visit.

We camped in Dillon, Montana, August 5–9. On August 6, the local Kiwanis club fed us breakfast and lunch; another thank you to the local folks taking care of us. We were able to use the local public library there in Dillon to check e-mail. A great help when on the trail and you cannot get a cell phone signal. We set up stations for visitors each day and manned them for the benefit of the visitors to our camp.

We camped in the shadow of Rattlesnake Cliff in Barrett, Montana, August 10–14. The cliff is so named by Captain Lewis because of the large number of rattlesnakes encountered by the Corps in this area. Our men had no such problem. The men of our Corps took an opportunity to swim and bathe in the Beaverhead River at this encampment. The air temperature was hot and the water was cool and swift, so the combination of these elements made for a fun activity. We were using Castile soap, which is the soap supposedly used in 1805. There is a soapstone plant nearby. This stone is refined to make talc. The stone is very soft and easy to work with when using the proper tools. Many of our men took large pieces of soapstone and fashioned them into pipes like the Indians did. As a matter of fact, Captain Lewis showed a diagram of an Indian pipe in his journal, which our men used as a model for their pipes.

August 12 was the commemorative ceremony of crossing Lemhi Pass, coordinated by the U.S. Department of Agriculture Park Service. The ceremony took place on Lemhi Pass, a beautiful day. There were about 200 people present for the commemoration. Several speeches were given and at the appropriate time, Captain Lewis (Bryant Boswell) and his men appeared on the east side of the pass. They walked to the center of the pass and gazed west. They could not believe what they saw. Instead of the free-flowing waters of the Columbia River, they saw an endless chain of mountains. Oh, how disheartening this must have been, after traveling so far, to be confronted with this awesome view. I wonder just for a fleeting moment if Captain Lewis thought of turning around and going back. We will never know. The Discovery Expedition of St. Charles was the honor guard for the day. After presenting the colors and performing their other duties, we set up stations in the Sacagawea Memorial Area of the pass, conducted business as usual, and spoke with the attendees about our travels. We were honored to have the George family represent the Lemhi Shoshones Indians and visit with us. It was their ancestors who were so instrumental in furnishing horses to the 1805 expedition in order for them to proceed on. A barbecue was offered to all who attended the ceremony. Following our meal and presentations, we packed up the stations and returned to Barrett.

August 13 found us at Clark's Lookout near Dillon, Montana. It is here at this limestone outcropping that Captain Clark made several compass readings that could be made today because the landmarks can still be seen. By triangulation, you could be standing in his footprints. It was quite an experience to know that you were standing where one of the members of the 1805 expedition actually stood.

On August 15, we arrived at our next campsite in Grant, Montana. We camped next to the Canvas Café. Today was our first day on horseback. The Diamond Hitch Outfitters provided fifteen horses for us. Since there were more than fifteen men in camp, not everyone could ride. Therefore, if you did not ride that day, you would ride the next. I did not ride that day. Some of our men who did not ride chose to walk the trail. I stayed in camp. We met the outfitters at Camp Fortunate, and consequently, today was about a nine-mile ride for our guys from Camp Fortunate to Grant. When the horses and riders arrived at Grant that evening, DeEsta Wellborn treated us to an old-fashioned Montana barbecue. Another thank you was in order.

On August 16, I rode a horse for the first time in many years. The non-riding crew moved our tents and the rest of our camp to James Ranch. The outfitters tried to size each of the riders to the appropriate horse, big men on bigger horses, and smaller men on smaller horses. Stirrups were lengthened or shortened as needed. Belly straps were tightened, and we were off.

We left Grant and proceeded to ride toward Red Butte, about nine miles' distance. Thank goodness, this outfitter furnished us with trail horses. Trail horses were trained to follow the horse in front of them. These horses did not go off in any direction trying to find new trails. It was rather comfortable letting the horse do his thing. I enjoyed the scenery because I was just along for the ride, and what scenery! Montana is Big Sky country. The hills, prairies, buttes, gullies, sagebrush, and tumbleweed all form an awe-inspiring, panoramic view. This was August and everything was parched brown, only in varying shades of brown that are difficult to describe. We rode to the top of a butte for an awesome view of the surrounding rangeland. We must have been 200–300 feet above the plain, which gives us a commanding view. As we sit atop this butte, we could only speculate where the exact trail was that the 1805 group took, but we can readily speculate that they were within sight of this butte. We descend the butte and rode till we arrived at James Ranch. There we camped for the night.

On August 17, the riders took the horses from James Ranch to Lemhi Pass. The non-riders moved the camp to Lemhi Pass, an elevation of 7,373 feet above sea level. We were granted permission to camp on top of the pass. Permission is needed because this is a restricted area for camping, as it is a National Historic Landmark. While in this area, we visited a rivulet similar to the one Private Hugh McNeal stood astride. He did this to declare that he stood astride the mighty Missouri River. The park service placed two, large, flat rocks on both sides of the rivulet to make it easy to take pictures. We do live in the twenty-first century. We had beautiful weather, great camaraderie, and a memorable sunset.

On August 18, I was on horseback again. But we had to go a short distance to meet the Rawhide Outfitters of Salmon, Idaho. Lemhi Pass is on the Continental Divide, and the divide is the state line between Montana and Idaho. Nowadays, we have too many laws. An outfitter licensed in Montana is not allowed to travel in Idaho, and an outfitter licensed in Idaho is not allowed to travel in Montana. Consequently, we had to change outfitters at Lemhi Pass. We bid farewell to the Diamond Hitch Outfitters and were welcomed by the Rawhide Outfitters. After mounting up, we rode fifteen miles down into the Lemhi Valley toward Salmon, Idaho, another interesting trip. As we descended into the valley, we were apparently following old Indian trails because the trail was well-worn. Once again, we had good trail horses because they just followed the horse in front of them; my kind of riding. As a sidebar comment, these outfitters charge about $80 per day per horse, multiplied by fifteen horses ... you do the math. I wonder what Captains Lewis and Clark paid for their horses during their trip?

A good question was raised. Where did we get the money to pay for this type of transportation? Part of the money came from selling t-shirts and other souvenirs in our traveling store, part of it came from individual and corporate donations, part of it came from fundraisers along the trail, part of it came from the local communities along the trail, part of it came from the outfitters who reduced their charges in order to help us, part of it came from our presentations in the Tent of Many Voices, and part of it came from grants from state and federal agencies. We were indebted to a lot of people and organizations who have helped us to complete this historic reenactment. After our fifteen-mile ride, we were transported to our campsite in Salmon, Idaho.

From August 18–28, we were camped in Salmon, Idaho. During our stay in Salmon, we had an open camp and set up stations for our visitors. We also worked closely with Corps of Discovery II: 200 Years to the Future and their Tent of Many Voices, as we did since leaving Elizabeth, Pennsylvania, in August of 2003. Corps II, as this traveling unit was known, was a mobile exhibit of the National Park Service. It followed the Lewis and Clark Trail since 2003, and our paths crossed many times. The women and men who accompany the exhibit were old friends of the Discovery Expedition of St. Charles. The Tent of Many Voices was an integral part of Corps II, because it was in the tent that hourly presentations were made for six or seven hours each day by very interesting presenters—from well-known personalities to local historians. The varied assortment of subjects presented was mind-boggling. The Discovery Expedition of St. Charles presented a fair share of diverse hourly subjects for the Tent of Many Voices, and we thank them for these opportunities.

Once again Private Hall was requested to post entries on the Discovery Expedition of Saint Charles' Web site in order to keep the men not on the river tuned in on our happenings and progress.

The journal entry follows:

Sunday, August 28, 2005
As seen through the eyes of Private Hugh Hall (Ed Scholl):

The day started in the middle of the night at 0445 hours with someone chopping wood. The sound of the ax splitting the logs was heard all through the quiet Lemhi Valley, disturbing all humans and beasts. Apparently, Lloyd Gower and Jerry Hebenstreit could not sleep and were taking their frustrations out on logs instead of people.

Reveille was 0600 hours followed by a breakfast of eggs to order, French toast, and bacon. At 0700, the flag was raised and the journal for the day was read by Captain Clark. No entry was made by Captain Lewis for this day and many days to come.

At 0800, we left camp to find our horses for the day's ride. Two hundred years ago, the expedition was in the Lemhi Valley following the Salmon River, just as we were doing. The sky was blue, the clouds were white, and the temperature was about sixty. Last night the temperature was forty-nine in the tent, since the tents are about ten degrees warmer than the outside temperature; the outside temperature was thirty-nine for a low. The high turned out to be ninety-three in the afternoon.

We met the Rawhide Outfitters a few miles above Tower Rock. The Rawhide Outfitters are owned by John and Cathy Cranny. This is the same outfit who furnished us with fifteen horses for our trip from the top of Lemhi Pass down into the Lemhi Valley. We found their trailers and were mounted and on our way by 1000 hours.

We had three wranglers with us. Each wrangler had a five-horse string. Justin and Luke were sons of John and Cathy, and the third wrangler was Shane. Yes, he was named after the famous 1956 movie *Shane*.

The horses were of excellent quality and trail wise, thank

goodness. We started up into the high country and traveled for two hours before stopping for lunch. The trail we followed was a winding narrow adventure toward a blue, blue sky. We climbed and climbed, and the horses sweated and sweated. We did not ride for a solid two hours, but we gave the horses a periodic break by walking them. The horses were surefooted, and when you gave them enough reign, they found their way over rocks, logs, gopher holes, horse dung, and roots. There were several places where we passed over rock outcropping and the horses slipped slightly but still kept their balance. I was riding Ed, a very tall, gray stud. He and I got along very well after I spoke to him and rubbed his nose and forehead and pulled on his ears before mounting him. He responded to the slightest tug on the reigns.

As we climbed out of the valley, the views became spectacular. Most mountains and hills in Idaho are brown, dry, grass with splotches of green pines on the sides and tops. I had asked a local if Idaho was ever green, and he said, "Yes! In May and June when the rains come." Now, in August, it looks like Idaho is a fire looking for a place to happen. As a matter of fact, a few days ago we were told that there were some twenty-six fires now burning in Idaho. There are days when the mountains, both near and far, are covered by a smoke haze. Some days the mountains are barely visible.

We rode for an hour or so without seeing a fence, just God's creation of Mother Earth. The views of the rolling hills, mountains, and valleys are almost beyond description. As you look down from the high country, you wonder which way is out. A rule of survival is to go downhill because you will eventually find water, and that leads to a river where people have settled. It does not pay to go to a higher point in the landscape because the view will be the same—only of a greater distance.

We stopped for lunch at 1200 hours and rested the horses for a little over an hour. The afternoon ride was another two hours. At one point of this ride, we rode along a trail that was about eight inches wide with a 200–300-foot drop and no guardrail. Thank goodness, horses have four feet. With the three wranglers, we had an eighteen-horse string. I was number fifteen or sixteen in line and ate trail dust all day long. Ed did not like trail dust either, and he would step out of line to get some fresh air when I was not paying attention. Since he and I were thinking the same thing, I let him breathe fresh air. I can now see why cowboys wear bandanas.

The afternoon was hot as the temperature rose into the nineties. At one point, we had a long, downhill trek. We dismounted and walked the horses for sometime. I understand that you don't ride a horse downhill because the saddle slides forward and throws the horse off balance. Since I did not want to ride between Ed's ears, I gladly dismounted. We walked, and walked, and walked. After a while, I began wondering why horses got a break but humans did not get breaks. We finally reached the bottom of the downhill trail and again mounted up. After ducking limbs and branches, we reached the trailers and said good-bye to the wranglers and horses. We walked a short distance to the highway and found a safe, drinkable spring. This is the only time in my life that I can remember cold spring water tasting better than beer.

We then drove to John and Cathy's house for dinner. They were most hospitable hosts. We were served roast chicken with delicious gravy, mashed potatoes, fruit-filled cranberry sauce, and whole-kernel corn mixed with black beans. Then desert came with cake and homemade ice cream, the end to a perfect day on the trail.

But wait, that's not the end. After spending four hours riding horses in ninety-degree weather, we were a bit grungy. Four of us decided to go to Sharkey's Hot Spring for a hot tub bath at 2000 hours. It was an outstanding decision. That hot spring was just what the doctor ordered. After being sore and tired after a day in the saddle, a hot tub bath was the end of a glorious day. I slept like a log for seven hours, and my body healed itself for the next day's adventures.

The next encampment was Tower Rock, Idaho, from August 29–31. Another Web page journal entry follows:

Monday, August 29, 2005
As seen through the eyes of Private Hugh Hall (Ed Scholl):

Today is moving day. We have been in Salmon, Idaho for ten days. We move to Tower Rock today.

Reveille is 0700 hours. Pack your personal gear, have a cold breakfast, drop the tents, load the trailers, and move to Tower Rock. All went as scheduled because we have been doing this since August 31, 2003.

No wood chopping at 0445 hours today, so no excitement before 0700 hours.

A local member of the Bureau of Land Management died. DESC was requested to have a presence at a memorial service for him. David Krosting, age fifty-one, died of cancer. Six members of DESC attended led by Captain Clark. They were Captain Clark, Ed Scholl, Dan Herman, Ed Falvo, Jason Ryberg, and Jack Simons. A very moving service.

Upon arrival at Tower Rock, some of the tents had already been raised by the men who did not attend the service. Camp was completed and lunch eaten.

At about 1400 hours, the Krosting family arrived at Tower Rock and distributed Dave's ashes over the Salmon River. Another moving service. The afternoon gave us free time. Moccasins were mended and made. Clothing repaired. Food purchased. Journal entries made. Naps taken. Flintlocks fired and cleaned. Baths taken in the Salmon River. Cars repaired. News exchanged. Stories and jokes told.

On August 31, we traveled to Hamilton, Montana, to participate in a rather large festival parade. We had some men in dress blues and some men in leather. The National Guard integrated us into their line of march. It was an honor to march with them in a now and then scenario. With the amount of applause we received as we marched through Hamilton, we apparently were well-received. Not historically correct, since we had our red pirogue with us. It was trailered and towed by a National Guard truck, our Jan Two Bears Falcon portrayed Sacagawea riding on the pirogue.

Moved our camp to Lost Trail Hot Springs, Montana, on September 1. We were there till September 3. We were back in Montana, and that requires an explanation. In the twenty-first century, the Continental Divide is the state line between Montana and Idaho. When we crossed Lemhi Pass, we crossed the Continental Divide and went from Montana to Idaho. In 1805, the Lemhi Shoshone Indians told Captain Lewis that there is no trail on which they could cross the mountains in this area. They would have to go north through the Bitterroot Valley to the Lolo Trail to cross the mountains. The Lemhi Shoshones gave the 1805 expedition an Indian named Old Toby to guide them. In order to get to the Bitterroot Valley from the Lemhi Valley, you must cross Lost Trail Pass (elevation 7,014 feet above sea level), which is on the Continental Divide. When you do, you are back in Montana because you have re-crossed the Continental Divide. The trail now runs for about 100 miles through the Bitterroot Valley till you reach Lolo Pass, which leads to the Lolo Trail. Now, Lolo Pass is on the Continental Divide, and consequently, when you cross Lolo Pass, you are back in Idaho. Get it? If not, a map may help you understand the geography of the area.

We were camped behind the Lost Trail Hot Springs Resort in a rather remote site. We had a reveille formation each morning to raise the flag and a retreat formation each evening to lower the flag. During the formations, we sang "Chester." The United States did not have a National Anthem in 1805. The Discovery Expedition of St. Charles adopted "Chester" as its official song for flag raisings. One morning, Hebe said that we should sing the "Party Song" at reveille when no one was around. All agreed. As the flag went up, an abbreviated "Party Song" was sung. Sergeant Ordway (Gary Ulrich) was flabbergasted. Captain Clark was aghast and ready to throw the journal he was holding into the fire. Sergeant Ordway said, "That was pretty funny, but don't ever do it again." Naturally, when composure was resumed, "Chester" was sung with gusto. All work and no play made DESC men dull boys.

The next encampment was Darby, Montana, from September 4–6. It was here that Pete Murray of Burbank, South Dakota, joined us for a week. In an effort to make him feel at home, I wore an Edgar's soda jerk hat to formation. Well, everyone laughed when I helped fold the flag at retreat, everyone that is except Sergeant Ordway. He said, "Okay, Hall. You are out of uniform and now have kitchen police today, tomorrow, and the next day." Some people have no sense of humor.

You might be interested in our kitchen police duties while on the trail. KP stands for kitchen police in the military. When on KP, you help the cook prepare meals and clean up after all three meals. We were on a military expedition, and therefore subject to all military regulations.

In an army unit, the First Sergeant keeps three duty rosters. One duty roster was for Charge of Quarters (CQ). The Charge of Quarters was on duty all night to answer any off-duty phone calls or respond to an emergency. Since we did not have a phone, we did not maintain a CQ roster. The second roster was a guard duty roster. We did have guard duty when on the Ohio River and on the lower portion of the Missouri River. Once we were in the sparsely populated Dakotas and Montana, we no longer maintained a guard duty roster. The third roster was the KP roster. All soldiers take their turn on all of these rosters when they are maintained. Officers, NCOs (noncommissioned officers), and cooks do not normally pull these duties. The rosters were maintained so that all personnel were treated fairly.

KP duties required that you be in the kitchen prior to reveille, in order to have coffee ready for the men. You must stoke up the fire for breakfast and heat three large coffee pots to make hot water. You throw a handful of coffee into one pot to make coffee. The last cup of coffee in that pot is pretty bad. One of the other hot water pots was for cereal such as warm oatmeal, cream of wheat, or for a cup of tea or cocoa. The third pot was used in the three rinse bowls. The first rinse bowl had hot water and a small amount of detergent in it. The second rinse bowl contained hot water and a mild amount of Clorox. And the third bowl had clear, hot water as a final rinse. These three bowls were prepared at all three meals.

We used pewter or wood bowls for eating. Coffee, tea, milk, water, soda, or beer was always drunk from a copper or tin cup of the early 1800 period. The KPs (usually two) scramble the eggs and cooked the bacon. The cook handles the pancakes on our flat grill. It was not unusual for the pancakes to have blueberries, crushed walnuts, or mushroom bits in them. The men had a choice of scrambled eggs and bacon, pancakes, warm or cold cereal (prepared by themselves), and many times cantaloupe or other fruit. Condiments were put out on the kitchen table. They included salt and pepper, butter, maple syrup, catsup, pickles, and anything else that a KP might find in the kitchen and the men would eat.

We fed from fifteen to thirty men three times a day. Cleaning up after these guys could be difficult. The spills were accidental. The men did not mean to spill milk or syrup, but it just happened. At the end of breakfast, the KPs put the unused cereal and condiments away and wash all the pots and pans and other utensils. The rinse bowls are emptied and dried to be used at the next meal.

The next meal was lunch. It was not unusual to have flat meat (sliced lunch meat) and cheese for lunch. Peanut butter and jelly was a staple. Potato chips were crushed on sandwiches along with pickles and hot peppers. When on the river all day, which happened quite often, sandwiches were made at breakfast. The KPs had to put all the makings, plus snacks and fruit, out at breakfast and then put everything away that was not used. Water coolers had to be filled with lemonade or ice water as needed. Trash and garbage was placed in plastic bags and disposed of in local containers. If no containers were available, we took our trash with us.

There was a rule in camp that there was to be no plastic or aluminum containers sitting around the camp. Our kitchen tent had a covered storage area at the back. All non-period items were placed in the storage area, out of view of the general public.

Sometimes we had soup or leftover stew for lunch. Consequently, the rinse bowls were necessary. At suppertime, the KPs made the salad, sliced the tomatoes, peeled and diced the potatoes and carrots (if needed), sliced the onions and peppers. We had many one-pot meals, such as stew, chili, chicken and dumplings, spaghetti with meat sauce, etc. On some nights, we had individual items such as hamburgers, steaks, mashed potatoes, green beans, anything the cook could dream up. But at the heart of it all were the KPs. Their work was determined by the types of meals being prepared. You can imagine the work necessary to feed thirty men three times a day. Unfortunately, not everyone likes the same thing. We did have some very finicky eaters. At supper, we normally had a dessert. This could range from store-bought cake to our own homemade banana cream pudding. Many times the locals brought us desserts. God bless them. The smaller the number of men, the easier it was on the KPs and the cook; but at the same time, the quicker your name came up on the KP roster again.

After dinner, a clean up was in order. The KPs put everything away that could be used or eaten the next day. Pots, pans, kettles, and utensils were cleaned, and some items were oiled with vegetable oil to prevent rusting. We cleaned out the rinse bowls again and set up the coffee pots for the next day. Every once in a while you would get lucky. This happened when we were invited out for lunch or dinner or both in the same day. If your name was on the KP roster for that day, then—as the saying goes—that was the way the cookie crumbles; or that was the way the ball bounces; or that was the luck of the draw; or God had smiled on you. After a day on KP, no wonder a soldier could use a cold beer. The flag is down, so let's start our campfire.

Traveler's Rest, Montana, was our next encampment, September 7–10. There we supported Mike Wallace and the Traveler's Rest Brigade, or Chapter of the Lewis and Clark Trail Heritage Foundation in commemorating the encampment in 1805. Archeological research has been done in this area. As a result of this research, it is recognized that this campsite is on the original campsite of the Lewis and Clark Expedition. One of the finds was the excessive mercury found in what was believed to be the latrine area of the original camp. The men had been treated with Dr. Rush's thunderbolts. This medication was heavily laded with mercury, and when passed through the men, it was deposited in the latrine. Another find was what was believed to be the central fire pit. Lead was found in the pit and believed to be lead melted for shot. Today, this area is a state park. We were camped in the park and did not have to use trench-type latrines. We do live in the twenty-first century. During our stay, we were visited by hundreds of schoolchildren and people interested in the Lewis and Clark adventures.

We spent September 11 at Lolo Hot Springs, Montana. This is a resort that has year-round teepees. We were able to sleep in the teepees rather than pitch tents. This was a welcome break.

Lolo Summit/Pass was our encampment for September 12–14, elevation 5,235 feet above sea level. On September 12, we were on horseback again. This time we were outfitted by the Triple-O Outfitters, owned by Barb and Harlan Opdahl. They became an integral part of our trip because they were with us for the next eight days as we crossed the Bitterroot Mountains on our way to Weippe Prairie and our meeting with the Nez Perce Indians. We had fifteen horses again, but still not enough for everyone to ride every day. We had a fifteen-mile ride today—as the crow flies. When you add in the up and down portions of the trail, it was more like twenty miles. We did go through landscape that was radically different than the Lemhi Pass area. In the Lolo Pass area, there are trees, and trees, and trees. As a matter of fact, you must be cautious of branches and limbs hitting you in the face as your horse finds its way through the heavy forest. There were times when the trail was quite wide and other times when it was overgrown. The horses were surefooted and quite capable of stepping over rocks, roots, holes, and other obstacles that were in the way. This made for a long and adventurous ride.

We arrived at Lolo Summit, as the interpretative center is known, or Lolo Pass, as shown on the map. The non-riders set up camp on the lawn area in front of the interpretative center. While there, we met Margaret Gorski, Carol Hennessy, and Katie Bump. They were employees of the United States Department of Agriculture (USDA) Forest Service and were our contacts for travels across the Bitterroot Mountains.

On September 14, General Mosley of the Montana National Guard arrived in a helicopter for the transfer of the espontoon. The espontoon is a spear-like device carried by a soldier. It became a symbol of authority. When transferred by a leader of a unit, it designates the recipient as the new leader of the unit. The espontoon was transferred from the Montana National Guard to the Idaho National Guard, which signified that they were the custodians of our welfare while in Idaho. This ceremony was conducted with much fanfare, as we were in formation with members of both the Montana and Idaho National Guard. The color guard was from the Montana National Guard. They were immaculately dressed and marched with precision, a well-choreographed presentation.

We traveled the Lolo Trail from September 15–19. On September 15, we were on horseback again. Several of our men started walking an hour ahead of the riders. We rode up over Wendover Ridge and were now onto the famous Lolo Trail. It was exciting to think that we were riding on the same trail that Indians had used for maybe hundreds of years and then to be used by the 1805 expedition. The area was heavily forested and visibility was limited by the trees. We had an uneventful ride until our horses disturbed a nest of ground bees. As the horses were being stung, they began to become unmanageable. After the outfitters determined what was happening, everyone was told to spur their horses out of the danger area. In a few minutes, we were back to a normal trail ride. Eventually we caught up with our walkers. We rode twenty miles and camped at Cayuse Junction.

On September 16, I did not ride. Our riders rode twenty-six miles, the longest trek on the Lolo Trail. As a non-rider I helped move our camp to Castle Butte Junction. We had a couple of four-wheeled vehicles that towed the trailers we used to transport our gear. I'll bet Lewis and Clark wished they had this kind of support. The Lolo Trail winds through forests and runs on top of the mountains. The Indians who first used this trail found it easier to stay on top of the mountains rather than following the rivers in the valleys, namely, the Lochas and Clearwater Rivers. The Nez Perce Trail also follows the tops of the mountains. Sometimes it is on the Lolo Trail, and other times it parallels the Lolo Trail. The Nez Perce used this trail to hunt buffalo on the other side of the mountains. One of the problems with mountaintop trails is snow. Any trail on top of a mountain is unusable for a portion of the year, depending on the snowfall that year. We were okay this year, but on our return trip in 2006, we were unable to use the Lolo Trail because of snow. In 1934, the Civilian Conservation Corps cut a road through the top of these mountains. The USDA Forest Service maintains the road today and has designated it as Lolo Motorway 500. Individuals may use the motorway if they obtain a special use permit issued by the Forest Service. The Lolo Trail crosses Motorway 500 at times but most of the time it parallels the motorway. In the afternoon, we stopped at the Indian post office. There is a cairn, or mound, of stones erected as a landmark here. There is no mention of such a marker in the journals. Consequently, it is conjecture that the cairn existed at the time the Lewis and Clark party passed by here in 1805 and 1806. Today it is a tourist stop for anyone traveling on the Lolo Trail. The view of the surrounding mountains is superb.

On September 17, I was on horseback. We rode eighteen miles. We did not see any game because our horses were snorting and kicking rocks and roots all day long. The trees had thinned. We could now see for miles, and there were many, many mountains ahead of us. But there appeared to be more mountains behind us than there were ahead of us. Living in the twenty-first century, I knew what was ahead. Can you put yourself in their place, not knowing what lay ahead or how far it was? The only thing they had going for them was Old Toby, their Indian guide. He knew the way and undoubtedly kept the captains informed of their progress. We arrived at Weitas Meadows before dark. The camp was ready and a meal was being cooked. Oh, the luxuries we had compared to 200 years ago.

On September 18, it was eight miles to the next camp at Boundary Junction. I was not on horseback. We had a forest ranger join us. He stopped our vehicles several times to show us interesting things about the forest. At one of the stops, he pointed out a path that was supposed to be the original Lolo Trail, believed to be over 200 years old. I have no doubt that it may have been because we are creatures of habit and usually use the same avenues and trails in our travels today. Furthermore, why climb over a tree or rocks when you can walk around them? We normally do take the course of least resistance, and I am sure that is what the moccasin-footed Indians did years ago.

On September 19, I was again on horseback. We could see Weippi Prairie in the distance, but it was still miles away. We had to go twenty miles to our next campsite at Lolo Creek. We were coming down off the top of the mountains. The trees were thickening and the trail was all downhill, which means walking the horses on steep grades. The trees were beginning to become much larger, which probably meant old growth forests. There was not much, if any, logging in this area. We finally came to Lewis and Clark Grove, where we popped out onto Motorway 500. Our ground crew was waiting for us. We dismounted for pictures in front of the USDA Forest Service sign. There were twenty-eight men present for that picture. We then continued our ride along the motorway for a short distance to our campsite at Lolo Creek. There was cold beer for everyone as we had completed our journey through the Bitterroot Mountains, an accomplishment even in today's environs. I had that warm inner glow that comes with a milestone accomplishment. How many people in today's society have had the opportunity to ride horses on the Lolo Trail? We in the Discovery Expedition of St. Charles feel blessed, and we should feel that way.

Weippi, Idaho, was our campsite from September 20–25. We established camp in Weippi, and then at noon reenacted the meeting with the Nez Perce Indians in a field on the Weippi Prairie. We were greeted and gifted by Ralph Johnson, a direct descendant of Wautkuweis, Allan Pinkham, a tribal elder and historian, and Gloria Johnson, also a descendant of Wautkuweis. Wautkuweis is the old woman who interceded for the expedition in 1805 by telling the Nez Perce Chiefs not to harm the white men because she had been treated kindly by other white men after they had rescued her. Our captains gifted the tribal representatives and sat down to smoke a peace pipe with them. This meeting was watched by about 200 spectators, videoed by several cameras, and narrated by Chuck Knowles, a noted, local Lewis and Clark historian. It was a very pleasant day in the field under a beautiful blue sky with wisps of white clouds. Eight men left camp and went home after the ceremony. That left more food for us at the community hall that evening, where the local residents had dinner for us. We were camped next to the Weippi Elementary School. Each morning, our formation would march to the school at 0800 and raise their flag while singing "Chester" as the kids stood at attention in front of the school, another warming experience that can only be experienced by being there. On the afternoon of September 21, we were treated to a buffalo sausage cookout with all the trimmings at the home of Ed and Marge Kuchynka. The Kuchynkas were the event planners for the Nez Perce reenactment meeting on Weippi Prairie on Tuesday. On September 22, Vicky Smith of I-Can provided dinner, and as usual, provided more food than we could eat. On September 23, three more men left for home. On September 24, we were treated to a chicken dinner at a local tavern, compliments of our Florida benefactor, Miss Rae. During our stay in Weippi, the entire elementary school cycled through our camp's stations. When they were not in camp, we had other schools cycling through. It was a great time in Weippi, Idaho. We thank you, Weippi.

We moved to Canoe Camp near Orofino, Idaho, on September 26, and were there until October 7. This is the same amount of time that the 1805 expedition spent in Canoe Camp. Like them, we made dugout canoes. However, we only made two dugout canoes, not five dugout canoes like they did. The Hog Heaven Muzzleloaders of Moscow, Idaho, provided two large ponderosa pine tree logs for our use. They also provided two already-made dugout canoes for our use. God bless the Hog Heaven Muzzleloaders because we did not have to make four dugouts. We did use the tools and implements used in the 1805 era, such as adzes, draw knives, axes, saws, wooden mallets, and other carpenter tools of the times. Since the original expedition had thirty-two men with them at this time, and we had sixteen men, I guess we did all right. Much sweat, tired muscles, aching backs, and other sundry ailments were experienced during these two weeks, but no serious injuries from these archaic tools, only blisters. When not working on the canoes, the men were making paddles. The primary tool for making paddles is the draw knife. When not working on the dugouts or making paddles, we were manning stations and speaking with the hundreds of schoolchildren who visited our camp each day. Our two canoes were finished on October 5. We were camped next to the Clearwater River, the only undammed river we traveled on across this vast country. White water and many rapids are in this natural river. All four dugouts were launched on October 6. We were once again waterborne and finally going downstream. And downstream we went, about a mile a minute, bumping over submerged rocks and I don't know what else. About two miles downstream were serious rapids, all bubbling, white, and ugly. I was in the third dugout and told to paddle hard as we went through the rapids to maintain control of the canoe. We followed the first two dugouts and made it through the rapids okay. The fourth canoe apparently struck a rock and turned over. The five men either hung onto the capsized dugout or made it to a rock. They were all recovered by the sheriff's water patrol boat. The canoe was recovered and beached a short distance downstream. We continued on for about twenty miles. The highway along the river was lined with spectators all clapping and cheering as we went by, another heartwarming experience, even though the water we were sitting in was cold. We beached the dugouts and went back to camp. On October 7, we were back on the river, and late that afternoon we arrived at the Corps of Engineers Marina in Clarkston, Washington. We returned to Canoe Camp and prepared for our move to Clarkston. That evening, we were hosted at a cookout by John Fisher and his neighbors in Juliaetta, Idaho.

October 8–10 was our encampment in Clarkston, Washington. We were at the confluence of the Clearwater River and the Snake River. The Snake River is a big, big river compared to the Clearwater River. We were in Washington State and met a Special Forces (SF) team from Alpha Company, 1ˢᵗ Battalion, 19ᵗʰ Special Forces Group of the Washington National Guard. The team of fourteen men were assigned to assist us in our travels down the Snake and Columbia Rivers. We did not know it at the time, but they would save our butts several times during the last 474 miles. They had four Zodiac pontoon boats, and we had four dugout canoes. All was well. We also met John Umbarger and his mate on their United States Coast Guard Auxiliary D-13 boat. They also provided an escort for us while we were on the Snake River, along with the Coast Guard Cutter Bluebell. Umbarger took us from our dugouts a couple of times in order to expedite our trip. We also met Chief Warrant Officer Terri Purcell, who was our liaison with the Washington National Guard. She was extremely helpful during this portion of our journey. While in Clarkston, we set up stations for the visiting public, had a presentation in the Corps II's Tent of Many Voices, participated in a veteran's recognition ceremony with the Idaho

National Guard in the Tent of Many Voices, participated in the passing of the espontoon ceremony from the Idaho National Guard to the Washington National Guard, were hosted at the Elks Club for dinner, and assisted in the closing ceremony for Corps II. All events went well and we were ready to get back on the river.

On October 11, we left Clarkston for Boyer State Park. We had to pack wet canvas because it rained all night. Wet canvas is dreaded because it is heavy, and when put up at the next camp, you are unpacking wet canvas and trying to erect wet, heavy, canvas tents. What a bear! This was about a twenty-five-mile trip in bad weather. We took three canoes because of a lack of men. We spent eight hours on the river. We ate soggy sandwiches for lunch. We were towed by the Zodiacs for a portion of the trip because we did not want to be on the river after dark. We did not have running lights on the dugouts. As you know, the Coast Guard requires boats to have running lights when moving on navigable waters after dark. We went through the lock on Lower Granite Dam. This is the first of four huge dams on the Snake River. All of them drop about 100 feet, which is about the height of a ten-story building, an impressive sight when traversing the locks.

On October 12, we were about eighteen miles from Central Ferry State Park. Weather was better—no rain, but the wind picked up. Paddle, paddle, paddle. The view of the hills, cliffs, rugged outcroppings, and rock formations made the trip interesting, although not enjoyable. I wondered if the men on the 1805 trip had the same feelings. Incidentally, during this Snake River increment, this was the Mike and Ed boat because the crew was Mike Dotson, Mike Bowman, Ed Falvo, and me, Ed Scholl.

On October 13, Lyons Ferry State Park was our next encampment, about twenty-six miles' distance from Central Ferry State Park. We locked through the Little Goose Dam on that day. As usual, we had to tie up to a motor-driven boat to go through the lock. We also had to exit the dugouts and get into the Zodiacs as we went through the lock, as per Corps of Engineers requirement. Once again, the 1805 expedition did not have to meet these requirements. Because of the distance, the Zodiacs lashed our canoes to their boats and towed us part of the way. We were going so fast that the dugout was taking on lots of water. Since discretion is the better part of valor, Captain Lewis (Mike Dotson) and I climbed aboard the Zodiac. It was a rough ride because the water was choppy from the wind. We trailered the dugouts there at Lyons Ferry State Park because of the almost sixty miles' distance to Sacajawea State Park, and we were due there early on October 14.

During October 14–17, we were camped at Sacajawea State Park in the tri-cities area. Pasco, Kennewick, and Richland, Washington make up the tri-cities area. This area is at the confluence of the Snake and Columbia Rivers. I thought the Snake River was big, but the Columbia River is huge, a formidable flow of water going to the Pacific Ocean that is now about 350 miles away. Sacajawea State Park was host to about 700 Boy Scouts and a trapper's rendezvous—quite a sizeable audience to keep our stations busy all weekend. We were hosted to a spaghetti dinner by the trappers/mountain men and Allen Berg and Roberta Manley of the Freedom Bell. I visited a leather crafter from Klickitat, Washington, at the rendezvous and had him make me a pair of moccasins. What was nice about these moccasins was that they were lined on the inside with sheepskin. This was great for cold weather. On October 15, a Special Forces soldier and myself attended a Coast Guard critique. It covered our cruise down the Snake River. John Umbarger gave a Power point presentation with some outstanding pictures. Everyone was satisfied with the past performances, and we discussed the problems we would face once we were through the four dams on the Columbia River. At that point, we would be in tidal water with the swells and currents that were inherent in these conditions. The short-range weather forecast did not look good.

We moved on to Irrigon, Oregon, for October 18 and 19. The

weather again was cold and wet. This kept the kids from visiting our camp. It was a slow couple of days.

We moved to Roosevelt Recreation Area, Washington, on October 20, a bad weather day. It was dismal and windy, and the river was very choppy, so much so that all of our dugouts were swamped. The Coast Guard Auxiliary came to our rescue. They took us out of our dugout, put us on their nice dry boat, and transported us to Crow Butte State Park, where we waited for ground transportation for more than two hours because Crow Butte was not one of our scheduled stops. Cell phones had their place on our trip. The swamped dugouts were brought in by the Zodiacs. When we arrived at the campsite, our ground crew had already set up camp. Sergeant Pryor (Norm Bowers) was with us on the boats. He slept in the orderly room tent. There was a huge commemorative rock just the right size to completely fill the orderly room tent. You guessed it. Our ground crew got the bright idea to pitch his tent over the rock. Of course, when he opened the tent, he was amazed. Taking it in stride, as you must do with this crew, he joined in on the good laugh.

We spent October 21–23 at Maryhill State Park, Washington. The weather finally broke, and we had some beautiful dry days. God owed us these days. Normally eastern Washington has a semi-arid climate, so much so that the surrounding hills are brown and dry at this time of year. The Columbia River gorge is absolutely beautiful, a must-see during your lifetime. I believe we were seeing it from an angle that most people do not see it from—that is river level. Looking at the hills and up at the cliffs and rocks made you feel kind of small. While at Maryhill State Park, we took in the sights, namely the Maryhill Museum and Stonehenge Memorial. Construction of the Maryhill Mansion was started by Sam Hill, a Quaker pacifist who envisioned a Quaker agriculture community around the mansion, but he died in 1931 before its completion. Consequently, upon its completion, it became a museum. The Stonehenge Memorial was also erected by Sam Hill as a tribute to the soldiers of Klickitat County, Washington who lost their lives in WW I. Since Maryhill State Park is located in a sparsely populated area of Washington, we did not have many visitors during our stay there. We enjoyed the downtime, dried out, relaxed, and spent our time mending and making clothes.

The Dalles, Oregon was our next encampment from October 24–27. We camped on the grounds of the new, beautiful Gorge Interpretative Center. There is an old building with a loft on the grounds. Several of us slept inside for those four nights. We manned Rock Fort while there with four men each day. The Special Forces also sent a couple of men each day to Rock Fort to have a presence there and speak with visitors. Rock Fort is a massive rock outcropping overlooking the Columbia River. In 1805, the captains thought that it would be easy to defend this location in the event of hostility, and therefore camped on the rock while they were there. The local community sponsored a fundraiser for us at the elks club. An excellent meal was presented with lots of cakes. The Dalles is on the east side of the Cascade Mountains. A couple of miles west of The Dalles, within a mile and a half, the terrain changes radically from barren treeless hills to forested hills and mountains. The change is unbelievable in such a short distance.

We moved to Viento State Park near Hood River, Oregon, on October 28 and into rain. We were packing wet canvas again. Then to Cascade Locks, Oregon for October 29–31, and three more days of wet, dreary weather. During the move, the boats were filling with water from the rain as we were paddling in very uncomfortable conditions. Our campsite was wet and muddy. One consolation was that we had the use of a covered, waterproof, large, gazebo-type structure. We could have meetings inside and stay dry. Another amenity was the use of the wireless Internet connection at the local motel. They were very accommodating at the motel. We thank them for their hospitality. We set up stations at our camp, but we had sparse crowds because of the weather. On October 30, we had a complimentary ride on the sternwheeler, Columbia Gorge, a very interesting and informative trip. It was overcast and misty, but not raining. We had 100 or so schoolchildren with us. Consequently, we had time to speak with some of them about our travels. It was a good day in spite of the weather. That evening, the local community furnished us with a salmon dinner. Things like this made for a bright day, even if the weather was not cooperating.

On November 1, we moved to Rooster Rock State Park, Oregon. The weather was so bad I went with the ground crew. It was raining and cold. The guys in the boats must have been freezing their butts off. We packed wet canvas again. There was no chance for the tents to dry in those few days. We were now below Bonneville Dam, which is the first dam on the Columbia River going upstream. That meant tidal water and all of the good and bad aspects that go with it. The good part was that when the tide was going out, we were paddling with it. But when the tide was coming in, we were paddling against it. We camped within view of Vista House, which is situated high on a cliff. The cliff affords a super view of the Columbia River Gorge, both up and down the river.

We camped on November 2 at Captain William Clark Park in Washougal, Washington. It did not rain. We set up stations and spoke with many of the local folks who visited our camp. They fed us a buffalo burger dinner. We had a large fire in a huge metal cauldron that the locals said was found in a field nearby. There was a large gathering of people around the fire. We presented an apology to two descendants of Chief Tumaulth, who was unjustly hung by the military in 1865. This was our effort to heal one of the injustices done to Native Americans in the past. The descendants, Sonny and Taylor Alvik, accepted our apology and gave us their blessings. It was a very moving and inspirational ceremony.

November 3 was spent at Frenchman's Bar Park in Vancouver, Washington, which is across the river from Portland, Oregon, which is about eighty miles from the Pacific Ocean. The dugouts were paddled eight miles to Frenchman's Bar in nasty wind and rain.

An oceangoing freighter was anchored in the river within sight of the park. The freighter was facing upstream when we camped in the park. Six hours later, the freighter was facing downstream. The tide had turned the freighter completely around. This happened about every six hours as the tides changed. We had heard so much about the tides in the Columbia River, and here was visual proof of the problems we were facing. The park was in a remote location. Consequently, we had very few visitors during our stay.

We moved to Kalama, Washington on November 4. I was on the ground crew today. It was another quiet day because our campsite was difficult to find. It was nestled among railroad tracks, industrial buildings, storage yards, and Interstate 5. The 1805 expedition did not have these manmade structures to worry about. They just pulled up on the bank and camped. A lot has changed in 200 years. That afternoon, Rex Becker and I went for a beer at a local tavern in Kalama. The uniforms we were wearing brought us into conversation with other patrons. One of the patrons was a towboat captain who was retiring that year after thirty-some years on the Columbia River. We had a very interesting conversation about the river, since he had been using it for so many years on a towboat, and we were using it in dugout canoes. He and two of his friends invited us to his home for a cookout dinner. The captain had an outstanding collection of hunting knives and Indian arrows. Much to my surprise, he gave me one of the homemade hunting knives to carry on the Lewis and Clark trail. It was little things like his kindness and generosity, that gave all of us on this reenactment memories we would never forget.

November 5 was spent at County Line Park, Cathlamet, Washington. I was on the ground crew again today. It was a very sunny day. We set up camp and dried out canvas tentage. That evening, we were hosted by Margaret Miller and her friends for dinner at her home. It turned out that Margaret and I lived in Erdenheim, Pennsylvania, at one time. As a matter of fact, she attended Springfield High School in Montgomery County. My two daughters also graduated from Springfield High School. Here she was, living in Washington State, and I was passing through with the Lewis and Clark Expedition, and our paths crossed. What a small world. Margaret became a good friend and member of the Discovery Expedition of St. Charles. We saw her quite frequently along the trail after this meeting. As a matter of fact, we stopped at her home again for dinner in 2006 on our return trip.

Vista Park, Skamokawa, Washington, was our next campsite on November 6. We paddled the dugouts to Vista Beach. It was nice to have sand at a landing instead of mud or rocks. The beach is quite wide—unusual for the Columbia River. It was a beautiful, sunny day. We finished drying our tentage. That evening, Rex Becker, Bob Anderson, and I went to a local tavern in Skamokawa for a beer. A hunter came up to our booth and said that if we helped him skin an elk, he would give us part of it. Without hesitation, I said, "Okay. Where is it?" Over the years I had field dressed and skinned lots of deer during Pennsylvania deer hunting season. I had never skinned an elk, but I thought that the principles would be the same. I thought that an elk must be like a white-tailed deer, only larger. I was right. He took us out to a barn that was next to the tavern, and there was the elk. It was tied to the forks of a forklift truck by its hind legs. I took my hunting knife and started to skin from the field-dressed rear quarter to the knee. The hunter said, "We don't do it that way out here. We ring the leg just above the knee. Then skin toward the belly. That way you get less hair on the meat." That was okay with me because there is more than one way to skin an elk. In a little over an hour, he and I had the elk skinned and quartered. True to his word, he gave us a hindquarter of the elk. We put the hindquarter in the car and took it back to camp. This was really a different evening. I can only imagine the members of the original expedition doing this hundreds of times on their three-year journey. They shot lots of deer, buffalo, elk, bear, horses, and other smaller animals, all of which had to be skinned in order to use the hides for clothing, moccasins, and bullboats. I am sure that all of the men became quite proficient in skinning animals. Their survival depended on it.

On November 7, we arrived at Knappton Cove Quarantine Station, Washington. The quarantine station was operated by the United States Government from 1899 to 1938 and was known as the "Ellis Island of the Columbia River." We were allowed to sleep inside the hospital building on its cots, beds, and floor. That beat a wet tent any time. While we were camped there, Gregg Parrott, who I believe worked as a butcher with his father, butchered the elk hindquarter for our kitchen. He did very well because when he was through, the only thing left of the hindquarter was bone. Naturally, we had elk stew and other elk dishes for several days.

"Ocian in view! O! the joy." One of the most famous phrases in American history. We arrived in the dugout canoes at Chinook Park, which is a mile from the location of Station Camp, on November 8 to end our epic journey to the Pacific Ocean. Station Camp is where the original expedition camped from November 15 until November 24, when they voted to cross the Columbia River and build Fort Clatsop on the south side of the Columbia River. We were welcomed at Chinook Park by Ray Gardner and other members of the Chinook Indian Tribe. The tribe members gifted us with salmon and a tribal flag. We gifted them with replica peace medals and an American flag. During our eighteen-day stay at Chinook Park, it rained, and rained, and rained. I don't believe we had more than two or three days of clear weather. Our Thanksgiving Dinner was eaten under shelters in order to prevent the rain from diluting the gravy. This meal and several others were prepared for us by Bob and Judy Andrews. The Andrews own a bakery/restaurant in Long Beach, Washington. We are indebted to them for these meals and all of the donuts they furnished us.

Visits to other historic sites were a must while we were in the area. The visits included but were not limited to: the Pacific Ocean, Fort Clatsop, Cape Disappointment Lighthouse and Coast Guard Station, Lewis and Clark interpretive centers, the salt works, whale bones, Clark's metal tree, Astoria Column, Forts Columbia and Stevens, Dismal Nitch, Station Camp, U.S. Quarantine Station, Astoria-Megler Bridge, Astoria Trolley, Flavel House, Netul River Trail, and the Columbia River Maritime Museum.

While at Chinook Park, I rented a house in Seaview for four nights. My daughter, Julie, drove down from Whidbey Island with the two grandsons, Ben and Jack. My daughter, Kate, flew up from Los Angeles, and we had a family reunion to celebrate the arrival at the Pacific Ocean. They participated in many of the festivities that occurred in the area and did their fair share of sightseeing, including flying Balsam glider planes off the top of the Astoria Column. It was a truly memorable occasion for everyone.

Fort Clatsop was destroyed by an accidental fire on October 3, 2005. This was just prior to our arrival in November. An archaeological dig was under way at the time we arrived. The National Park Service living history staff was presenting a primitive encampment symbolic of the camp prior to the building of Fort Clatsop in 1805. Several of our Discovery Expedition of St. Charles men were invited to participate in this presentation. Both units melded perfectly. It was a typical showing of camaraderie among reenactors we met in our travels across the country.

Thus ended our eight-month journey from Fort Mandan to Fort Clatsop. We disbanded for the winter and reassembled in March for the trek to St. Louis in 2006. That would be another six months on the river. But wait, I had to arrive home safely from this portion of my journey. That meant driving from Astoria, Oregon to Philadelphia, Pennsylvania, some 3,000 miles. The trip was not uneventful. Such are the trials and tribulations of the modern-day Lewis and Clark re-enactors; they are not too far off from their trials and tribulations.

The Fourth Leg of Four

March 23 to September 23, 2006

We were about to begin the final leg of our epic journey. Just like the original expedition, we retraced some of our footsteps to St. Louis. The exceptions were the Forgotten Trail and the trip down the Yellowstone River.

The following table gives you various locations of the 1806 expedition during their journey home. It also documents our stops on our journey home.

Recorded 1806	Recorded 2006
Mar 23 Left Fort Clatsop	Mar 23 Left Fort Clatsop, OR
	Mar 24 Vista Park, Skamokawa, WA
	Mar 25–26 County Line Park, Cathlamet, WA

	Mar 27–30 Frenchman's Bar Park, Vancouver, WA
	Mar 31 Marine Park, Vancouver. WA
Apr 3 Explored the Willamette River, (Portland, OR)	Apr 1–5 Capt Wm Clark Park, Washougle, WA
	Apr 6–7 Rooster Rock State Park, OR
Apr 11 Difficult time with rapids	Apr 8–12 Cascade Locks, OR
	Apr 13 Viento State Park, Hood River, OR
	Apr 14–15 Lyle, WA
	Apr 16–18 The Dalles, OR
	Apr 19–20 Maryhill State Park, WA
	Apr 21–22 Roosevelt, WA
	Apr 23–24 Crow Butte State Park, WA
	Apr 25–26 Irrigon, OR
Apr 27 Camped near the Walla Walla River	Apr 27–29 Sacagawea State Park, Pasco, WA
	Apr 30– May 4 Lewis and Clark Trail State Park, Waitsburg, WA
	May 5–8 Hells Gate State Park, Lewiston, ID

May 14-Jun 14 Camped at "Camp Chopunnish" near Kamiah, Idaho because of snow in the mountains	May 8 Corps Disbands
	Jun 12–18 Corps Reassembles at Lewis and Clark State College, Lewiston, ID for Summer of Peace National Signature Event
Jun 30 Arrived at Traveler's Rest Jul 3 The party splits	Jun 19–Jul 4 Traveler's Rest, Lolo, MT
	Jul 5 Lost Trail Hot Springs, Sula, MT
	Jul 6 Cross Gibbon's Pass to Hogan's Cabin
	Jul 7 Dr Loge's Ranch at Jackson Hot Springs
	Jul 8–9 Camp Fortunate, MT
	Jul 10 Barrett, MT
Jul 11 Lewis at the Great Falls Clark at Twin Bridges	Jul 11 Twin Bridges, MT
	Jul 12 Lewis and Clark Caverns, MT
	Jul 13 Three Forks, MT
	Jul 14–15 Livingston, MT
	Jul 16–19 Thompson Ranch near Big Timber

Jul 24 Clark on the Yellowstone River	Jul 20–25 Pompeys Pillar, MT (Clark on the Yellowstone National Signature Event)
Jul 25 Clark at Pompeys Pillar	
Jul 27 Lewis at Two Medicine and Confrontation with the Blackfeet	Jul 26–Aug 6 Yellowstone River, MT
Aug 3 Clark at the Confluence of the Yellowstone River and the Missouri River	
	Aug 7–9 Yellowstone Confluence, ND
Aug 11 Lewis shot by Cruzatte	Aug 10–13 Trenton Lake State Park, ND
Aug 12 The parties reunite at "Reunion Point"	
Aug 17 Charbonneau, Sacagawea and Colter leave the Expedition	Aug 14– 20 New Town, ND (Reunion at the Home of Sacagawea – National Signature Event)
	Aug 21–22 Fort Mandan, ND
	Aug 23 Whetstone Bay, SD
	Aug 24–28 Yankton, SD
	Aug 29–31 Burbank, SD
	Sep 1–3 Ponca. NE
	Sep 3–4 Sioux City, IA (Sgt Floyd Monument)
	Sep 5 Decatur, NE
	Sep 6 Wilson Island State Park, IA

	Sep 7 Omaha, NE
	Sep 8–9 Plattsmouth, NE
	Sep 10 Nebraska City, NE
	Sep 11 Rulo, NE
	Sep 12–13 Atchison, KS
Sep 14 Received whiskey, biscuits, onions, and pork from traders going up the river near Leavenworth, KS	Sep 14 Ft Leavenworth, KS
	Sep 15–16 Kaw Point, KS
	Sep 17–18 Lupus, MO
	Sep 19 Jefferson City, MO
	Sep 20 Washington, MO
	Sep 21–22 St Charles, MO
Sep 23 The Corps Arrives at St Louis	Sep 23 St Louis, MO (Lewis and Clark Currents of Change—National Signature Event)

I arrived at Fort Clatsop on March 20, after a five-day drive across the country. It was great meeting my fellow crewmembers again. About twenty men arrived in camp over the next several days. Camp was set up at Netul Landing, which is about a mile from Fort Clatsop. It is believed that when the expedition arrived here in 1805, they decided to build Fort Clatsop nearby. We were camped on a bed of gravel, which made for uncomfortable sleeping. The weather was damp, cold, windy, and there were constant showers. Apparently, we would be packing wet canvas for the foreseeable future. I couldn't wait till we got to The Dalles.

Over the winter, one of our men, Dick Brumley, built a Chinook canoe. He had the blessings of the Chinook Tribe to reproduce one of their canoes. These types of canoes are the ones that the Chinook Indians used to visit the expedition when they were stranded on the Dismal Nitch in November 1805. Captain Clark was amazed that the Indians could navigate the swells, waves, wind, and currents in this kind of weather when his dugouts were unusable under these conditions. Our Chinook canoe was tested and found as seaworthy as any of the Chinook Tribe canoes.

The next day, March 21, we trailered our canoe to Long Beach, Washington, for a cleansing ceremony. It was raining and cold. We and the other spectators were sheltered under a medium-sized nylon overhead on a boardwalk. Our canoe was placed on the sand dunes overlooking the Pacific Ocean, a very tranquil scene. Ray Gardner, vice chair for the Chinook Indians, proceeded to explain how a tribal canoe became a part of the tribe. The canoe protected all who traveled in it, and the canoe had a heart. Consequently, it had to be treated with respect. All impurities in the canoe had to be washed away. The ceremony consisted of a prayer and the use of cedar boughs to cleanse the canoe. As if with divine guidance, the rain stopped, and all crew-members proceeded out to the canoe. Each of us was given a cedar branch, and we walked around the canoe in single file, cleansing all parts of the canoe, inside and outside. The boughs were then burned in a fire to destroy all impurities, and this made the canoe a purified member of the tribe or expedition. The canoe was then given its tribal name of *Its Woot*, which means "Black Bear." In retrospect, *Its Woot* lived up to its expectations and served us well on our journey up the Columbia River to the Forgotten Trail. Following the ceremony, we had lunch at the Cottage Bakery, owned by our friends, the Andrews, saw the sights in Long Beach, and then had a very pleasant dinner and evening at Kris Manguson's beach house.

The following day was filled with preparations for our departure from Fort Clatsop. We assisted our fellow reenactors at Fort Clatsop float their dugout canoe that was mired on a mud flat near the fort. With personal equipment mended and made ready for the departure, our stores were acquired, inventoried, labeled, and packed. We keep our firewood covered in inclement weather so we could have our nightly campfire, if it didn't rain. We had our last campfire at Fort Clatsop that evening and started singing our favorite songs from previous years. What a pleasant way to start a six-month trip home.

Departure day was dismal and overcast with rain off and on just like 200 years ago. Not much has changed in 200 years. Fort Clatsop was destroyed by fire in October 2005. Following the fire, an archeological dig was mandated to determine if the present fort was on the footprint of the original fort. No conclusive proof was found to definitely state that the replica fort was built exactly where the original fort was built. But it is close enough to warrant the reconstruction of a replacement fort where the replica fort once stood. Consequently, a reconstructed fort was built in time for our departure ceremonies. The fort was complete except for the roof. We marched into the fort and had many speeches by well-wishers. We lowered the fort's flag, raised a flag belonging to one of our men to say that his flag had flown over Fort Clatsop, replaced the fort's flag, and smartly marched out of the fort. We were halted, told to fall out, and help dedicate the new Fort Clatsop-Netul Landing Trail. A dedication was held, and we walked the trail with the other spectators at the dedication. Upon arrival at Netul Landing, we were met by representatives of the Netul Tribe. They gifted each of us with a can of salmon, a jar of their tribal blueberry jelly, and a roll of toilet paper. These Indians know the necessities of life. We gifted them with tobacco and peace medals. The Chinook canoe was loaded along with the Fort Clatsop dugout canoe. I was assigned with three other men to man the dugout, an unfortunate assignment. After about three minutes following launching, the dugout began to leak. If someone had told me that this dugout had been used by the original expedition, I would have believed them. We were lucky to have a gallon plastic milk jug in the dugout. Apparently, the men who used the dugout yesterday had the same problem, hence the bailer in the dugout. The farther we went, the more water leaked into the dugout. We really had only three paddlers because one man was continuously bailing to keep us from swamping. Luckily, we only paddled about a mile and then went ashore. The Chinook canoe continued on down the Lewis and Clark River, across Young's Bay, into the Columbia River, under the Astoria Bridge, and on to Pier 39 in Astoria. We exited the dugout with our uniforms covered in mud because this is the dugout that had been mired in mud and not properly cleaned out before being used. Oh well, even a bad experience is an experience. It gives you something to talk about when it is over.

We went back to Netul Landing, picked up the vehicles and convoyed to Pier 39. We met the men who paddled the Chinook canoe and had a feast hosted by Floyd Holcom, a former member of the Special Forces unit who shepherded us down the Columbia River last year and the present owner of Pier 39. Pier 39 is a former salmon cannery. Holcom is refurbishing the pier for commercial use as offices. I am not a big Dungeness crab fan, but the word was that he had some fifty pounds of Dungeness Crabs, along with many, many other dishes available for this buffet. Quite a few local dignitaries, including our friends from the Special Forces, were invited to this feast. Our sleeping accommodations were indoors for the night. I spent the night with six other men, sleeping in a huge former walk-in refrigerator. I mean *huge*. Each of us had about 100 square feet to ourselves. Remember, this is a former salmon cannery. What a difference to sleeping in a tent with three other men. Plus it was dry. God has truly smiled on us.

March 24, and I was not on the river today. I helped move camp to Vista Park, Skamokawa, Washington. There was a very wide beach at this park, which was unusual for the Columbia River. The sandy beach was as wide as fifty yards. The Chinook canoe had a later start today because of the tide. They left Pier 39 at about three p.m. and had a fifteen-mile paddle. They ran into troubles with the tide and current. We were waiting for them all afternoon. It turned dark and they still were not at camp. We placed three cars on the beach facing downstream and turned on the headlights. Well into darkness, the canoe arrived, being towed the last five miles by a Zodiac boat. The men had a hot meal, donned dry clothes, and enjoyed a warm fire with a sing-along. The beer fairy had visited camp today, so all was well.

We moved camp to County Line Park, Cathlamet, Washington, for March 25–26. There was no river movement because of strong winds. Margaret Miller invited us to her home again for an outstanding array of hors d'oeuvres. We had the same invitation last year as we traveled west to the Pacific Ocean. We made a meal out of these delicacies and socialized with her neighbors and fellow canoe club members. Her home has a beautiful view of Mount Hood from the rear of the house, which overlooked the Columbia River. She followed our adventures and visited our camps on numerous occasions. Our campsite was in tight quarters. This park was squeezed between the Columbia River and a very steep precipice. The park did have adequate restroom facilities and much information and many pictures about the fish caught in the area.

Frenchman's Bar Park near Vancouver, Washington was our next stop from March 27–30, a much more spacious setting, with beautifully manicured lawns for camping. Weather was spotty. There was some sun in the morning and then showers in the afternoon or during the night. In Vancouver, we had access to their library's Internet service and showers in their community center. We also visited Fort Vancouver Historic Site, Clark College, Pearson Air Museum and restocked our supplies from local merchants. We had a unique experience at the Beaches Restaurant. Five or six of us went to the beaches for dinner. We had about a ten-minute wait for a table. During our wait, we were speaking with the hostesses, who had lots of questions about our period uniforms. When we were seated, they gave us a menu with the daily specials, which welcomed us by name to the restaurant. I was really impressed by this sort of treatment. It seems as though the management at the beaches printed the menus while we were waiting for a table. Quite a unique way to greet patrons. Roger Wendlick was with us at the restaurant. Wendlick is a noted historian with regard to the Lewis and Clark story, a former member of the Board of Directors for the Lewis and Clark Trail Heritage Foundation, who portrayed George Drouillard and lives in Portland, Oregon. Portland is just across the river from Vancouver. Following dinner, we were all invited to Wendlick's house to see the Lewis and Clark paraphernalia he had assembled. He had quite a collection of maps, documents, and a Jefferson Peace Medal which was struck from the same mold, as were the original peace medals. Weather was wet and cold, so no campfire upon our return to camp. It was a very dismal night. The following morning, about seven of our men visited the Washington State School for the Blind in Vancouver. With blindness comes a hands-on experience for touching our uniforms, furs, hunting knives, canteens, regimental buttons, bullets, hats, and anything else that we had with us. It was a very moving experience for the men who participated. That afternoon, we visited the Cathapotle Plank House near Ridgefield, Washington. These plank houses are mentioned in the journals and could house up to eighty people per house. The one we visited is a replica of the originals. As we crossed the tracks to enter the village area, we met about a dozen students from the Washington State School for the Deaf, who were leaving the village. Talk about a coincidence—here we are speaking with blind children in the morning, and by chance speaking with deaf children in the afternoon. The teachers accompanying the deaf children signed all of their questions and our answers, another moving experience for the men of the Discovery Expedition of St. Charles doing the Lewis and Clark reenactment. I feel so privileged to have been able to participate in this adventure. My life is full of chapters, but this chapter is ranked among the top three.

On March 31, we moved camp to Marine Park in downtown Vancouver. The weather was drizzling rain. So what's new? I couldn't wait till we got to The Dalles. We were invited to lunch at Jim Drew's home. Drew was the deputy sheriff who had been accompanying us in a Washington State Police and Rescue boat. He had helped us on several occasions ferrying crewmembers to and from the boats for one reason or another. His presence on the river gave us a safety factor, even though we were wearing or had access to life jackets. His home was of the log cabin-style with a porch all the way around the house. Gas grill cooking was on the porch. We were blessed with greasy, gooey hamburgers, hot dogs, and the usual staples of potato salad, chips, pickles, and soft drinks. A fun-filled afternoon. Just remember, in 1806, the locals fed the Corps. So why not in 2006? We then returned to Frenchman's Bar and had a three-hour paddle to Marine Park in light rain. There was no campfire.

Be alert, today was April Fools' Day. April 1, to be exact. The normal gags were done during breakfast, such as, "Your hunting knife is missing," "Your fly is open," "The milk is sour," "We are out of coffee," etc. Nothing was taken seriously, even when the sun was out, which happened for a short time during the day.

We moved camp to Captain William Clark Park, Washougle, Washington, for five nights. I was not on the river, but the boat crew started at six a.m. because the tide was right and reached Washougle at two p.m. An eight-hour run on the river. Our bread and butter stations were set up (weapons, uniforms, medical, and artifacts). Quite a few people visited our camp since it was not raining. That evening, a campfire was in order, and the usual singing was heard late into the night.

The next day, it was raining. Even so, about ten of our men took the Chinook canoe and went to explore the Willamette River in Portland, Oregon. This was the same day that Captain Clark and a group from the Corps did the original exploration. It seems as though on the trip west the Corps missed the Willamette because it was behind an island. On their return trip, they decided to explore the river. Our schedule had us exploring the Willamette in the rain. A soggy camp equals few visitors. What a difference a day makes.

The next day was full of sunshine and consequently drying ground. There were many visitors again until the shower in the late afternoon. Then more drying again. We were able to use a local wireless Internet connection at the public library.

The following day saw intermittent rain, and in the evening a showing of a National Geographic Lewis and Clark Film at the local high school. This was followed by a question-and-answer period for the good town folks attending the presentation, a worthwhile evening to follow one of our mandates, which is the telling of the Lewis and Clark story to as many people as possible. It was very interesting to hear the types of questions from the audience. They ranged from questions on the historical aspects of the journey to our present day adventures. This was of never-ending interest for me. Quite often at a gathering like this, we were asked to line up, give the people or audience our name, where we were from and who we were portraying. This is very apropos when a community feeds us. Normally we sang for our supper. We did two songs quite well. They were "Kentucky Women" and "Shenandoah." Depending on which men were with us, we did have solo performances of "The Lewis and Clark Rag" and "Ghost Riders in the Sky." Also depending on circumstances, "the Party Song" could be added. The local community and media had advertised a super campfire for our last night at Washougle. We could not disappoint them, and again, as if by divine providence, we had a clear evening. The campfire was lit, the crowd assembled, our Corps did its thing, our individual members did their things, and once again, a memorable night materialized. I wish I had purchased a recording system to capture these unbelievable evenings. We all had pleasant memories of these campfires, and we couldn't wait for the next one.

The next morning we packed camp for our move to Rooster Rock State Park, Oregon, for two nights (April 6–7). I was on the water today. It was a short trip of over five miles. We made the trip in two-plus hours. The weather was very cooperative today, no rain during our trip. Camp was already set up by the time we arrived with the boat. The campsite was named after a huge rock and sat beneath Crown Point. Crown Point and its Vista House, built in 1916, sat on top of a cliff which was two or three hundred feet high. This gave you a commanding view of the Columbia River Gorge both upstream and downstream. Looking upstream, you could see Beacon Rock which was mentioned in the journals. Looking downstream, you could see Washougle. Other points of interest in the area that we visited during the next two days were Multomah Falls, Horsetail Falls, Bridge of the Gods, old U.S. Highway 30, which snakes along the walls of the gorge and the fish ladders and their relationship to the Columbia River at the Bonneville Dam Visitor's Center.

The counting of migrating fish was quite interesting. As the fish climb the ladders (which were pools or steps along both sides of the dam) they were channeled into a passage that was illuminated, and each fish could be counted and tabulated as to size and type for migration purposes.

The next day we awoke to hollowing wind, and the river was a mess. Safety first dictated that there would be no water movement. We hunkered down in hopes that the wind would abate, but no luck. As a matter of fact, the wind was just as bad the next day. Consequently, we decided to trailer the boats to Cascade Locks for a five-day stay.

We broke camp in the rain on the April 8 and went to Cascade Locks, Oregon. We set up camp in the rain at the Cascade Locks Marine Park. I couldn't wait till we got to The Dalles. This stop put us above Bonneville Dam and consequently out of tidal waters, one less hazard to worry about in our travels upriver. Another benefit of the campsite was the use of a fair-sized octagonal building in our camping area. The building was dry and had electricity, a good place to hold meetings and set up our stations. The rain finally let up in the afternoon.

We were invited to attend the Spring Salmon Festival at the new longhouse in Celilo Falls Village the next day. The village was a short hour's drive from Cascade Locks. Upon arrival at the village, we were impressed by the size and newness of the longhouse. The building was oval in shape, had large windows in the slanted roof, was three stories high and a hundred feet long. We entered into a cavernous room that did not have any obstructions from one end of the room to the other end. A concrete floor about ten feet wide rimmed the interior of the building while an oval earthen floor was in the center of the room. Our guide was Dale Wheeler, of the Wynam Tribe, who helped us find a seat on the floor and explained some of the happenings. You could not sit anywhere you wanted. There were certain areas reserved for chiefs, elders, privileged guests, drummers, and other dignitaries. Men sat on one side of the room, and the women sat on the other side of the room, as was their custom. When we entered the room, there were over 100 people in the building and others still coming. We found our niche. Speeches were made outlining the importance of this ceremony. Prayers said, songs sung, and an order of precedence presented for the uninitiated. Women and children danced in the earthen oval for some time to the beat of the drummers. Then the women placed mats on the concrete floor and proceeded to bring in dish after dish of food. Most of the dishes were traditional in style, with other dishes being of a non-traditional nature. I'll list the dishes I can remember, and you separate them. Grilled salmon, elk and venison, potatoes, bitterroot, wapato, potato salad, squash, green salad, corn, huckleberries, pie, lemons, watermelon, and some dishes I can't remember. This was all washed down with water and soft drinks. About 200 people were served during this meal. Following the meal, all the men filed out of the east door, followed by the women, and walked completely around the longhouse. After everyone was once again gathered by the east door, final prayers were said, parting handshakes, and hugs were given.

We were then invited into a much smaller arena next to the longhouse. Here was where our leaders gifted the tribal chiefs and elders. The drummers in the longhouse had moved to this arena. We were then invited to participate in an honor dance presented by our hosts. Following this dance, we were entertained by men and women in their ceremonial attire consisting of beautiful feathers, beads, and colorful clothes doing various types of dances. This was an outstanding learning experience for all of us.

The following day was a down day with a few visitors coming to our camp. But the next day, we were inundated with schoolchildren and took a ride on the Sternwheeler Columbia Gorge with the kids. We had a captive audience, or did they have us captive? They out numbered us ten to one. We did not want to interfere with the information being presented by the sternwheeler's captain, so we answered questions during the captain's pauses. The weather was overcast and dismal, but no rain. When we docked, the kids poured into our campsite and visited the various stations we had set up. After the buses left, we were hosted to a dinner in the octagon pavilion by the friendly residents of Cascade Locks. They were very interested in hearing about our experiences. Consequently, we proceeded to inform them of many of our adventures, another instance where we sang for our supper. It was an enjoyable evening for all attending.

On April 13, we broke camp and moved on to Viento State Park, near Hood River, Oregon, for one night. I was on the ground crew. The boat crew had about a twenty-five-mile paddle. Dismal weather and overcast again, or should I say "still" but no rain. It was a normal day. Reveille at seven a.m., breakfast at seven thirty, formation with flag raising at eight (this included the daily reading of the journals), struck tents immediately following the formation, loaded vehicles, convoyed to Viento, set up tents and stations, had lunch, made presentations to visitors, repaired or made new equipment (moccasins, paddles, etc.), helped prepare dinner, retreat formation with flag lowering, dinner, campfire, and self-induced entertainment. Finally, sleep at your leisure. Somewhere during the day, you found time for errands and sightseeing, just so long as the stations are manned. Clearance with Sergeant Ordway was required to leave camp. After dark, the two-man rule was in effect. That was, you cannot leave camp by yourself. You must have a buddy with you. We have settled into this routine for so long that each man pulls his weight and everything runs efficiently. Peer pressure and the threat of kitchen police keeps thing running smoothly. I loved this military regimentation. I didn't have to worry about what to wear. It was the uniform of the day. We ate at seven thirty a. m., noon, and six p.m. . If you were not there at those times, you didn't eat. I loved it. The only real decisions during the day was what songs to sing around the campfire at night. What a life!

We moved to Lyle, Washington, on April 14 for two nights. We had a minor glitch when we arrived at Lyle. Our designated campsite was locked. Apparently, the park personnel were not informed of our arrival. Mindy, the owner of a small local restaurant, met us at the gate and did some resourceful thinking and research. She finally told us to camp on the field next to an unused elementary school in downtown Lyle. The field was quite large since it had a couple of baseball diamonds on it. This location was fine because the school was opened for us to use the showers inside. We set up camp and then went back for the boat. We had about a nine-mile paddle. The weather was okay in the beginning, but the wind picked up later that afternoon and presented some minor problems with wind-driven swells. After arrival at Lyle, we were invited to a dinner meal at the Cougar Den. Cougar is the Washington State University mascot. Incidentally, the restaurant was owned by our new friend, Mindy. She fed us a lasagna dinner at the restaurant. How do you thank people for those wonderful gestures of kindness? In most cases, a handshake or a hug was all that they were looking for. We had plenty of those and didn't mind sharing them. I am so proud to be an American.

The town of Lyle had an Easter egg hunt scheduled for this schoolyard the next day, which was Saturday. We had stations set up, and at nine a.m., the kids were ready for the hunt. Lanes were marked on the field and age categories were assigned to the various lanes. Many pieces of chocolate candy, plastic eggs with winning numbers on them, and other sweets were seeded in the yard. This small town certainly knew how to treat their children to a good time, and the dentists loved it. When the mayor blew the horn, it was a wild scramble by 100 or so little people having a wonderful time. We did too. Just watching the kids running in all directions was entertainment for us. As would be expected, the hunt was over in almost seconds, as the kids were like little vacuum cleaners, sweeping up the goodies into their Easter baskets. Naturally, we had many visitors at our stations all day.

That evening, we were hosted to a dinner at the Eagles Club in The Dalles by Allen Berg and his Freedom Bell friends. The dinner was a fundraiser for our Corps. I have no idea if enough money was raised to cover expenses, but the buffalo meal was great. This included the six, big birthday-type cakes depicting various stages of our trip pictured in the icing. A barrel of beer was tapped for our benefit. Naturally, we were called upon to introduce ourselves, and we again sang for our supper, another memorable evening.

During the evening, I spoke with Carolyn and Craig "Rocky" Rockwell. They were from Clarkston, Washington. Rocky worked for the United States Army Corps of Engineers, and at times portrayed Captain Clark. Carolyn made world-renowned brandied peaches. I didn't remember where on the trail I first tasted her brandied peaches, but when I told her how good they were she later left three jars of them for me in camp. I was off on a mission when she and Rocky delivered the brandied peaches. I am, to this day, indebted to Carolyn for her generosity and life-sustaining nectar of the Gods. Thank you, Carolyn.

The next day was Easter Sunday, and we attended an outdoor sunrise service in freezing weather. If it had rained, it would have been snow; it was so cold. A Methodist Church across the street from the schoolyard held the service. We had been invited to the service the day before. The parishioners were very friendly and fed us breakfast in the basement of the church, after the service. Since we had an early up, we had an early start to move our camp to The Dalles.

From April 16–18, we camped at the Columbia Gorge Discovery

Center and Museum, located in The Dalles, Oregon. We slept in a building which was built in the spirit of a mid-1800s farm building. There was a loft in this building, and some of our men slept in the loft. The loft reminded me very much of Fort Mandan because there was a loft in that Fort in which the men of the original expedition slept.

The Columbia Gorge Discovery Center and Museum has an outstanding display of Lewis and Clark memorabilia and Wasco County history items. It is worth a stop if you are in the area. About five miles west of The Dalles, you were leaving the Cascade Mountains when traveling east. In about a mile and a quarter, the trees end and the land became nude, an unbelievable change in the flora and weather. The Cascade Mountains are a natural barrier to the weather coming in from the west. Consequently, there was a semi-arid region from The Dalles to the Rocky Mountains which was about 200 miles east of The Dalles, an amazing transition of the landscape. Using hindsight, we did not have any rain for three weeks after reaching The Dalles. This was the reason that I couldn't wait till we got to The Dalles. Our tents were finally able to dry out. God had smiled on us again.

This was Easter Sunday, Carol Barnum and several of her friends brought an Easter dinner out to our camp. We met Carol last year on our travels west. She and her friends prevented us from starving to death on this beautiful Easter Sunday. Our period pewter and wood bowls were not large enough to hold the complete variety of foods she provided. Consequently, seconds and thirds were in order. The traditional ham, turkey, and chicken were served along with all of the traditional vegetables and condiments. Strawberry shortcake and a chocolate cake were included in the fare. There was enough food for forty people. Since there were sixteen of us, we ate Easter food for the next two days. No cooking—hurray!

We were visited by about 150 school students on Monday. They split their time between our camp and the Columbia Gorge

Discovery Center and Museum. Allen Berg also joined us with his Freedom Bell trailer and exhibit, a very active day for everyone.

Things settled down on Tuesday, and we had time for showers in the center and museum. Some of the men went to Rock Fort since they had not seen the Fort last year on our travels west. A carload of us went to Horsethief Lake State Park to see the ancient petroglyphs and pictographs. There were quite a few of each that could be seen near the parking lot, and a self-guided tour was available. It is another worthwhile stop when in the neighborhood. The Indian village where the 1805 expedition stayed is now under the water formed by the lake behind The Dalles Dam. Things have changed in 200 years.

We departed The Dalles on April 19 for a two-night stay at Maryhill State Park, Washington. We had been bouncing back and forth across the Columbia River, but that was exactly what the original expedition did during their travels. I was on ground crew. We moved and set up camp in the same location as we did last year.

Two points of interest in this area were the Maryhill Museum and Stonehenge. Both built by Sam Hill, a railroad tycoon. Mount Hood could clearly be seen because of the beautiful weather. The blue sky was a perfect backdrop for the white, snowcapped volcano.

There were a few trees at water level, but as you climb up to the tableland, the trees disappeared. Not much cultivated ground, but lots of grazing land for cattle. The ranches in this area were huge. The high gorge walls were behind us. There was a gentle, sloping hill at water's edge for about a quarter of a mile, and then a steep hill rising several hundred feet to the tableland on top. Once on top, you could see rolling, undulating hills for miles and miles. The stark nakedness of these treeless, rolling hills is unforgettable. A vast contrast to the tree-covered gorge walls in the Cascade Mountains.

Not much wildlife was seen; a few birds at river's edge, but no deer, elk, coyotes, or other wild animals. I believe the lack of tree cover had a lot to do with their habits.

Now domestic cattle were another story. The hillsides were dotted with grazing cattle, all kinds, colors, and sizes. The vastness of this tabletop terrain allowed for many head of cattle to populate the ranches, but they did not seem to be overtaxing the feed. All of the cattle had an ear tag. I presume it was used for tracking their heredity. A lot has changed in 200 years, and a lot has remained the same.

We did not have many visitors because of the remoteness of this campsite. Our four stations were set up for the few locals who did pay us a visit. We again made our own entertainment with the campfire rituals.

In our second day at the park, Ray Gardner of the Chinook Tribe visited us and performed another cleansing ceremony for *Its Woot*. We all used cedar boughs and burned them after the ceremony. The canoe had served us well. We immediately put the canoe in the water and did a nine-mile paddle, just to stay in shape. The men then trailered the canoe and convoyed back to camp, except for Josh Loftis and me. We went back to camp in Jim Drew's Police and Rescue boat. Drew accompanied us on the water whenever we were on the river. It was nice to have him around.

We were very appreciative of the Washington State authorities for allowing Drew and his rescue boat to assist us while we were on the Columbia River. The beer fairy visited our camp, so all was well. Remember, the original corps had thirteen kegs or barrels of whiskey in their supplies when they left Camp DuBois. The wind came up during the night and collapsed one of our tents. The ridgepole broke. The wind continued into the next day, and we had to cancel a river movement because conditions were too dangerous.

We moved to a recreation area near Roosevelt, Washington, on April 21 for another two-night stay. We joined a rendezvous already in progress. A couple of dozen mountain men had pitched their tents along with a half a dozen traders/vendors. The mountain men were very glad to see us and made us feel welcome. That evening they prepared the meal consisting of buffalo and elk stew and beer. Consequently, we had another amazing campfire gathering, especially when the mountain men joined the festivities. A visit to the traders' tents was in order. They had many things that you don't find at Walmart, such as, moccasins, string leather (in many colors), rattlesnake skins, period hats and hat bands, period bandanas, flints for muskets, replacement period hunting knives and sheaths, period clothing, furs, fire-starting steel strikers, etc. Apparently, the rendezvous was well advertised locally because we had a couple of bus loads of schoolchildren visit us along with many other interested local residents. On our second day at this campsite, we even had some old friends visit: the Matthews family from Washougle, Roger Wendlick from Portland, and Allen Berg and Roberta Manley, of the Freedom Bell fame, from The Dalles. Allen and Roberta brought several buckets of fried chicken with them, a most welcome gesture. The more people the merrier because it just adds to a bigger and better campfire gathering. We were furnished with plenty of wood. This enabled us to keep a fire going into the wee hours of the morning. It is amazing how much talent you can find at a rendezvous because the participants are all in period clothing and have some knowledge of history, stories, and songs that were told and sung around campfires a couple of hundred years ago. We heard some new verses to some of our songs, and they heard some new verses to some of their songs. That is what these gatherings are all about. Friendship and camaraderie abound.

Our camp moved on April 23 to Crow Butte State Park, Washington, for another two-night stay. This island was familiar because it was here that we were deposited in '05 after being rescued from our swamped dugouts by the Coast Guard Auxiliary. The park gets its name from a rather large hill that gave you a commanding view of the local area from the top. Several of our men climbed to the top and were impressed by the panoramic view. It was a couple of down days for us after all the excitement from the last few days. We had to trailer the boats to Crow Butte because the wind had kicked up in the morning and forced cancelation of a planned twenty-five-mile paddle. After setting up the tents, we fell into a normal day's routine. Four stations were set up and manned for the benefit of visitors. A few people came by, but not more than a couple of handfuls. The next afternoon, Bob Brown, the state Forest Ranger assigned to this park, presented us with a case of wine from a local winery just up the road. Now we must not only take into consideration the feeling of the beer fairy, we must also be nice to the wine fairy and consider her feeling upon presentation of her gifts. We did not want to hurt either one's feelings. Consequently, we gladly accepted their gifts. The campfire gathering was quite lively that night. No court-martials were needed because the men behaved themselves.

We broke camp on April 25 and moved to Irrigon, Oregon. We launched the Chinook canoe and paddled the last nine miles into Irrigon. We set up camp in the same park as last year and prepared for schoolchildren tomorrow. Weather was still beautiful. No rain. The townspeople were very generous and easy to work with. We had access to the Internet at their public library. The next day we had over 300 school kids come through camp. The school buses must have been shuttling the children for that number of children to inundate us all day. The stations we manned were uniforms, fire-arms, medical, fire starting, Chinook canoe, and artifacts. It was a fun day. The evening meal was brought to camp by one of the local ladies. Another testament to the generosity and friendliness of the people we are meeting on our journey. Once again, we sang for our supper because we had a rip-snorting campfire that evening, a pleasant way to end a busy day.

April 27 was to be our last day on the river because we were approaching the Rocky Mountains. Camp was to be moved from Irrigon, Oregon, to Sacagawea State Park in Pasco, Washington, till April 29. Pasco was in the tri-cities area. The tri-cities are composed of Pasco, Kennewick, and Richland and were at the confluence of the Snake River with the Columbia River. The tents and other paraphernalia were packed and ready to move. But since this was our last day on the water, everyone was given a chance to paddle. There were two legs to this trip, a three-mile paddle and a twenty-mile paddle. I choose the three-mile leg. We launched the Chinook canoe at Hat Rock, which was above the McNary Dam. Hat Rock was mentioned in the journals as a landmark on the Columbia River. We paddled three miles upriver and then changed crews. My crew took the vehicles and convoyed to Sacagawea State Park. The new crew took the boat to the Walla Walla River and then trailered the boat to Sacagawea State Park. We actually had three boats with us, the Chinook Canoe and two dugouts. Our problem was having enough men to paddle all three boats. Normally we used nine or ten men in the canoes and six to eight men on ground crew. Consequently, we only used more than one boat when we had enough men to paddle and act as ground crew. Our numbers changed because of men coming and going almost daily. Our men would volunteer days as their private lives dictated. Many of them were still employed and consequently could only make limited commitments. After paddling the twenty miles, the other crew arrived in camp late in the afternoon. The tents were all set up and dinner was prepared. It was a bittersweet ending to our river journey west of the great mountains. But wait, the flag is down, and it is now party time. And party we did. The merriment continued long into the night. Early up next morning because we expected lots of visitors today, and lots of visitors did arrive all day long, including many homeschooled children. We made time to go into town to visit Walmart, the post office, Internet sources, and laundries. Then we had a dinner of venison fajitas and guacamole.

The nightly campfire was lit, and we began our ritual. This was the night that I had a run-in with Captain Morgan and Sheriff Drew. It was after dark when someone started passing a bottle of Captain Morgan Rum around the fire. When the bottle came to me, I wanted to see if it was really firewater. So, I took a mouth full, stood up, bent over the fire, and spit the liquid into the fire. It was firewater because a huge ball of flame came up and enveloped my head. Those sitting around the fire were aghast. Luckily, no singed eye brows or eye lashes, just a brilliant flash of light. That was the first dumb thing I did that night. The second dumb thing was to unceremoniously tell Sheriff Drew to back off. I was in the process of expounding on the relationship of radar calibration and a speeding ticket when Sheriff Drew tried to interject a point before I was through. Well, being the gentlemen that he was and knowing that no evil intent was found in statements made around a campfire, he politely backed off. When I was through, he proceeded to tell us about little-known facts relating to police radar. Campfire gatherings are wonderful places to be enlightened. It was another late, late night and tons of fun.

Our last day in the park was less hectic than yesterday; still busy with visitors, but not as many as the day before. As the day wore on the heavens became dark and overcast. In the late afternoon, the wind blew so hard that a gust picked up the Chinook Canoe and rolled it over two or three times before coming to rest against an upright charcoal grill. The men in the area ran to retrieve the canoe. We carried it to a sheltered area behind some trees and staked it down. We then had to re-erect a tent which had blown down. No campfire tonight because it was a restless windy night. In the morning, the weather cleared and we were off to Lewis and Clark Trail State Park in Waitsburg, Washington.

On April 30, we were ready for a five day encampment at the Lewis and Clark Trail State Park. The 1806 expedition camped in the vicinity of the confluence of the Walla Walla River with the Columbia River. The Indians told the captains about an overland trail to the Nez Perce Indian Villages. The expedition had left about fifty horses with the Nez Perce the year before while the men went down the Clearwater River in dugout canoes. This trail was referred to as the Forgotten Trail or a good road. If you were traveling east on the trail, it was also known as the Nez Perce Trail. If you were traveling west on the trail, it was known as the Celilo Falls Trail.

Whatever you call it, it saved the 1806 expedition about eighty-two miles distance by bypassing the Snake River. As the crow flies, it was about ninety miles from the tri-cities area to Lewiston, Idaho, but one hundred and twenty-one miles by road.

Since we no longer were using boats, we were back on horseback, just like 200 years ago. But things have changed in 200 years. The original trail had all but disappeared and was intersected with fences. I was very disappointed in the trail because we rode our horses on macadam highways and shoulders of roads, not the pristine beauty we experienced in the Bitterroot Mountains.

The Touchet Valley was beautiful in its own right, but heavily populated with ranches and farms. Camp was set up in Lewis and Clark Trail State Park, near Waitsburg, Washington. The amenities were fine because we had firewood, water, showers, and restrooms readily available. Our outfitter, Clod Miller, met us with his horses, and we were ready for tomorrow's ride.

At the campfire that evening, we were serenaded by a local teenager, Mariah Barthlow. Any visiting musician was welcomed to our campfires because they would always add something different and usually original to our festivities.

Up early the next morning and we rode along the Touchet River for a short distance, then up from the river to a road. We rode along the shoulder of the road till lunch. We ate our lunch at a location near where the 1806 expedition camped for the night. We continued along the road to Bolles Junction. We met Clod Miller there and trailered the horses for their trip back to a corral. We had steaks that night for dinner. Mariah Barthlow and her mother again joined us around our campfire. There were several additional local town folks joining us for our sing along. We never got tired of these nightly gatherings but rather looked forward to them.

The next day, May 2, was full of activities. Up early, we drove to Waitsburg, Washington, for a great all-American welcome. The population of Waitsburg was approximately 1,200 people. It seemed as though all 1,200 residents were in the town park to welcome us. The fact that the town closed the schools for the day probably helped. We formed up and marched to our seats in front of the podium. We were greeted by the mayor, who read a proclamation stating that today is "Lewis and Clark Day." A barbershop quartet sang a couple of songs. Then a school pep rally band played marching music. A pastor gave us his blessings. Each of us were gifted with a bag that contained candles made locally, a box of L & B Kitchen's Wheat Berry Chili made in Waitsburg, Washington, and a beautiful hardback copy of the town's history. Several other dignitaries made remarks as well as our Captain Clark. Upon completion of this exemplary Waitsburg welcoming, we marched about a block north to our horses and rode out of town. This was a short ride today of seven miles to our campsite at Lewis and Clark Trail State Park.

We had a quick flat meat lunch and then drove to Dayton, Washington, for additional festivities. The Dayton schoolchildren presented a Lewis and Clark musical in front of their historic train depot, quite a production for these grade school kids. They were awesome. After the musical, we were asked to introduce ourselves. Following our introductions, we sang our signature songs of "Kentucky Women" and "Shenandoah" and socialized with the kids and town folks till three p.m.

At three p.m., the town had planned a three-mile walk from the depot to the Patit Creek Campsite. The Patit Creek Campsite was where local historians believed the 1806 expedition camped on the night of May 2, 1806. This campsite was just east of Dayton. The town had erected thirty-eight life-size steel cutouts depicting the Corps and some of their horses at one hour before mealtime and darkness. It was a very impressive display and worth a stop when you are in the neighborhood. Upon arrival at Patit Creek Campsite, the good folks of Dayton had a cookout for all attending the festivities. A campfire was lit, and many people joined us for our nightly ritual. A handful of our men slept under the stars at Patit Creek that night while the rest of us went back to our tents at Lewis and Clark Trail State Park.

The next day, we met the horses at Patit Creek Campsite for a ride toward Pataha, Washington. We basically followed Highway 12, but did take some frontage roads on this fifteen or twenty-mile ride. The ride took us up onto the tablelands, where we saw rolling hills and farmlands for miles. We also visited gigantic modern-day windmills. Then we went down through the Tucannon Valley and up the other side where we met Clod's horse trailers. The horses were corralled in Pataha for the night while we were corralled in the Lewis and Clark Trail State Park. We then had another campfire with Mariah playing her fiddle for us.

May 4 was our last day for horses on the Forgotten Trail. We mounted up at Pataha, rode the shoulder of Highway 12 for a while, and then took a farm road on the left up onto the tableland again. We were now away from the traffic on Highway 12, a much safer and relaxing ride. The terrain was still composed of rolling hills and farmland, but you could now see those snowcapped mountains just waiting for us.

The distant mountains were very majestic and beautiful as we stared at them. We had no idea of the problems we were about to face as we tried to cross them.

Our ride today was comfortable and very scenic. The horses just plodded along. It was a bit hot, as the sun was out and the temperature was probably in the eighties, but we were traveling east, and that was the direction to home. Every clip-clop of the hooves brought us a step closer to St. Louis. I wondered if this was what the men of 1806 were thinking. We took another farm road and came down off a ridge to where the horse trailers were waiting. The horses were unbridled and put into the trailers. We bid our farewells to the outfitter and drove back to camp.

This was our last night at Lewis and Clark Trail State Park, so it was party time. The locals seem to know this also because there was a very nice turnout of visitors for our campfire. We had buffalo stew for dinner. Mariah and her fiddle were back to help us with our farewell sing-along.

Gary Lentz, Park Ranger, host for Lewis and Clark Trail State Park, and a local Lewis and Clark expert was also present. His expertise and boundless knowledge about the Lewis and Clark story had him in high demand for presentations in the local area. It was a pleasure to have had him with us as a Lewis and Clark enthusiast. We presented him with one of our crew medals for his help during our stay at Lewis and Clark Trail State Park. He was a most deserving recipient of the medal.

We moved camp to Hell's Gate State Park in Lewiston, Idaho, on May 5. As we entered the park, we saw a lush, green, flat camping area near the river, but we were directed to set up our camp on a knoll overlooking the river. The knoll was barren of grass, rocky, covered with dry vegetation, and many piles of horse manure. The area was used as a trailhead by riders who unloaded their horse trailers in this area. Since we were going to be there for a night or two, we made the best of it. We did have access to shower facilities and restrooms, and that was a plus. The next day, we performed necessary errands and found Internet connections in the local community.

A National Bicentennial Signature Event was scheduled for Lewiston, Idaho, for June 14–17. The Discovery Expedition of St. Charles had been invited to participate in the event which was entitled, The Summer of Peace: Among the Niimiipuu. The signature event was scheduled to be hosted by the Nez Perce on the grounds of the Lewis and Clark State College in Lewiston, Idaho. In an effort to get a heads up on our future campsite, several of our men went to the college and surveyed our future camp location. We then had an outstanding meal with salad and steak. A steak dinner was reserved for special occasions. This was a special occasion because we were getting ready to disband for a month.

When the 1806 expedition arrived at the Nez Perce village, the Lolo Trail was impassable because it was snow covered. The 1806 expedition camped with the Nez Perce Indians during the month of May, 1806, because the Nez Perce refused to furnish the expedition with guides for the Lolo Trail.

Rather than our camping for a month, before attempting to use the Lolo Trail, our corps disbanded and the members went home.

We reassembled on June 12 at the Lewis and Clark State College Campus for the National Bicentennial Signature Event. The signature event was hosted by the Nez Perce and was well presented. We had set up our tents and displays and were blessed with good weather for a week. Consequently, many people visited our campsite. The Hog Heaven Muzzleloaders, of Moscow, Idaho had several of its members assisting us with presentations.

The Nez Perce presented drummers with dancers, storytelling, demonstrations of arts and crafts, traditional games, and vendors selling their arts and crafts and traditional foods.

A symposium was conducted in the college, with many of the leading Lewis and Clark scholars and historians making presentations.

On June 14, the United States Army 3rd Infantry Regiment's Fife and Drum Corps made a presentation on the Lewis and Clark State College's baseball field. Their performance was preceded by a presentation made by the Nez Perce Nation Drummers. The Discovery Expedition of St. Charles, under full arms and accouterments, escorted the fife and drum corps onto the field. Then we lined up between first and second base and second and third base giving the fife and drum corps a backdrop for their entrance and presentation. We saluted the fife and drum corps with a present arms and then smartly marched off the field, leaving the fife and drum corps to put on a spectacular performance. Their precision, music, and accentuated movements were mesmerizing. It was a truly memorable day for the hundreds of spectators in the stands. What helped to make this display outstanding was the fact that the fife and drum corps was meticulously dressed in white and red Revolutionary War era uniforms, and we were dressed in tattered brown leather clothing, duplicating the garb worn by the Corps of Discovery at that time in 1806. What a contrast!

At the conclusion of the Summer of Peace National Bicentennial Signature Event, we were in touch with members of the United States Department of Agriculture Forest Service about crossing the Bitterroot Mountains using the Lolo Trail. Just like the 1806 expedition, we were told that we could not use the Lolo Trail because it was impassable due to heavy snow still blocking the trail. Since we were on the 1806 timeline, we packed up camp and convoyed to Traveler's Rest which is in Montana.

This trip took us through an absolutely beautiful and impressive Clearwater and Lochsa Rivers Valley. I wondered why the Indians took the high road when crossing the Bitterroots until I saw the underbrush, fallen trees, rocks, steep banks, rapids, and other impediments to using the rivers as a means of travel. The Indians did the right thing by crossing on the top of the mountains. Upon leaving Lewiston, Idaho, we entered the Clearwater River Valley. Then at Lowell, Idaho, the Lochsa and Selway Rivers met to form the Middle Fork of the Clearwater River. From this point on, we were in the Lochsa River Valley. The valley is still beautiful, even though it changed names. After several hours of driving, we climbed to Lolo Summit and then down the other side of the Bitterroot Mountains to Traveler's Rest.

We arrived at Traveler's Rest on June 19 and were there until July 4. We were met by our old friends of the Traveler's Rest Brigade and warmly welcomed. We set up camp on the footprint of our previous encampment. Here in Lolo we had restrooms, showers at the local fire station, Internet connections at Park Headquarters, laundry facilities, and security by local law enforcement.

Each day we were committed to sending a contingent of men to several locations for local commitments. The first commitment was Southgate Mall. Here we set up stations in the mall and marched through the mall on an hourly basis, singing our marching songs. The merchants loved it, and the shoppers applauded us as we marched by. There were vendors in kiosks in the mall selling merchandise appropriate to the Lewis and Clark Story. It was a very festive week planned by the local community.

Another commitment for personnel was at the Rocky Mountain Elk Foundation. Here, a display of period tools and equipment was set up, and we were asked to help man the presentations on a daily basis.

Historic Fort Missoula had a presentation during our stay at Traveler's Rest, and we were asked to furnish men for their parade.

A monument to Captain Lewis' visit to the Missoula, Montana area in 1806 was restored and rededicated. Our corps was out in force for this rededication.

We also had to maintain enough men in camp to man our stations and speak with visitors. We were drawn quite thin by all of these requests, but the men were happy to do so. It gave them something to do during the day instead of sitting around camp and repairing clothing and equipment.

Trading off on assignments was also a break in our routines. Unfortunately, there was an open fire ban in Montana at this time because of the dryness hazards. Consequently, we could not have our nightly campfires. But this does not deter us from gathering around a blanket and having a good old-fashioned Indian trading session. At one of these trading sessions, a person puts something on the blanket that they would like to trade. Everyone around the blanket had a chance to examine the item and then puts something in front of him or her that they would like to trade for the item. It was not unusual to have a half a dozen items put on the blanket for trading. The owner of the original item had the option of examining all of the offered items and then selecting the one that best interested him, or takes the item back if he was not satisfied with what was offered. With twenty-five people gathered around a blanket, the trading could become quite lively.

Toward the end of our stay at Traveler's Rest, we were invited to

Elk Creek, Montana, for a cookout. There were four or five direct descendants of the men on the original expedition living in Elk Creek, and they wanted to meet us. Nine of us went to the cookout and had buffalo burgers with all the trimmings. It was a super afternoon because our hosts treated us like royalty.

Alas, it was now July 4, and time to leave Traveler's Rest. We packed our camp for movement. Our Captain Lewis took five men and headed for Great Falls (In 1806, Captain Lewis took nine men with him. We did not have enough men in camp to be historically correct). Captain Clark took the rest of us, and headed for the Yellowstone River. I chose the Yellowstone River because I had been on the Missouri River last year and wanted to see what the Yellowstone River was like.

We arrived at Lost Trail Hot Springs, Sula, Montana, on July 5. We set up camp and spent the night at the same location as last year. We were now out of the "no open fire zone" and had our campfires again.

I would like to remind you that the original Expedition had thirteen barrels or kegs of whiskey in their inventory when they left Camp du Bois on May 14, 1804. They did not run out of whiskey until they reached the Great Falls on July 4, 1805. Soldiers have been known to have a beer after the flag goes down. Private Hall had a reputation to maintain.

Early the next morning, July 6, we met the outfitter with our horses at Forest Service Road 106. Forest Service Road 106 goes through Gibbons Pass, elevation 6,941 feet, which crosses the Continental Divide, and then down into the Big Hole Valley.

The road was dirt and very rustic. There were no vehicles seen other than the one or two Forest Services vehicles looking out for our welfare. What a super ride! We were again in the forest and on trails that wound through heavy brush and open ground. Just like mountains should be—not following the shoulders of macadam highways. The horses were trail horses and used to following in a string. The pace was slow, and therefore the ride was enjoyable.

We left the road and followed trails that narrowed to a path. Branches were an ever-present danger because the horse's heads are lower than the rider, and it was not unusual for a rider to fend off branches at eye level. The horses were sure footed, as long as you gave them some reign, they found their way over rocks, holes, roots, fallen limbs, and any other obstacle in their way. There were times when a horse slipped on a rock and stumbled. This woke you up quickly. The shade of the trees added to the enjoyment of the ride. We stopped about every hour or so and gave the horses a rest. Since we were coming down off the top of a mountain, we usually walked the horses on steep inclines. This was done to prevent you from sliding forward with the saddle and ending up on the horse's ears. The problem of a saddle sliding forward can be prevented if there were a rump strap on the horse, but not all horses have a rump strap.

Lunch break was taken at about noon. Four hours in the saddle necessitated a butt break. We were now down in the valley and near water for the horses. The horses were allowed to drink, but not like a camel, just enough water to refresh them. The wrangler watched and told you when to pull their heads up.

The trees thinned as we came down the mountain. Near the top of the mountain, there was a dense forest with huge trees and many, many downed trees to walk around. Halfway down the mountain, the forest started to open up. There were not nearly as many trees. At the bottom of the mountain, there was water and fields with open meadows. The landscape had changed dramatically. We were now crossing the Big Hole Valley, and there were many more open areas than forested areas.

As we crossed the valley, we entered the area where the Nez Perce Indians had the confrontation with the United States Army in 1877. It is now a holy place for the Nez Perce Nation.

Our destination was Hogan's Cabin. After crossing much of scenic Big Hole Valley, we reached the cabin in midafternoon. We dismounted, corralled the horses, and waited for our ride to camp. Hogan's Cabin was somewhere in the Big Hole Valley. There were no landmarks. So, unless you grew up here, you had no idea where you were or how to get out of the valley.

The cabin had not been lived in for fifty years. There was old furniture in the cabin and on the front porch. There was a modern corral. Consequently, someone was using the ranch rather frequently, but there was no one around. Our vehicles showed up, and we drove to our camp which was a short distance away for the night. The ground crew had already erected the tents. Dinner was made, eaten, and we all recounted the experiences of the day around the campfire. It was a super day in the saddle.

On July 7, we met our outfitter near Wisdom, Montana. We mounted up and headed for Jackson Hot Springs. This was a twelve mile ride on a dirt road. The ride was not nearly as adventurous as the day before. We were over the mountains on flat terrain and all the water ran downhill to St. Louis from this point on. "O! the joy!" After an uneventful ride into town, we tied up the horses, invaded the Jackson Hot Springs Lodge, had a cold beer, and were fed a super meal at the lodge, courtesy of the local town folks. God bless them.

We were also given a personal tour of the hot springs mentioned in the journals, which are now on private property.

After dinner, we convoyed to Dr. Loge's Ranch for our encampment. We quickly erected our tents. The ranch was a couple of miles south of Jackson Hot Springs. The doctor and his wife were wonderful hosts. They gave us the run of their new beautiful ranch house, which had running water and a shower.

The next day, Dr. Loge took us for a short walk to a rise near his home and pointed out the location where it was believed that an 1806 encampment was made. Before leaving for Camp Fortunate, we presented Dr. Loge and his wife with crew medals and thanked them for their hospitality. This was another example of the people along the trail inviting us into their lives and homes. The generosity of the American people was unbelievable.

We moved to and set up camp at Camp Fortunate, Montana, for

July 8 and 9. Camp Fortunate received its name on August 14, 1805, when Captain Clark, coming up the Beaverhead River, met Captain Lewis and the Shoshone Indians, who were waiting for him. It was here that the river split into two un-navigable streams. The dug-outs were then useless. It was "fortunate" that the Corps had finally met the Shoshones. The Shoshones were the first human beings the men had seen since leaving Fort Mandan on April 7, 1805. They had traveled over a thousand miles during that time period. The actual meeting site was now under water. The Clark Canyon Dam had changed the topography of the area.

In 1805, the corps left their dugouts there before they traveled over the Bitterroot Mountains and in 1806 they recovered their dug-outs for their trip downstream. Our campsite was in a remote area of the Clark Canyon Reservoir Recreation Area; therefore, we did not have visitors.

On July 8, we traveled to Lima, Montana to participate in an afternoon small-town welcome for the Lewis and Clark Expedition. We set up stations and spoke with the people who visited our area. The local community hosted us for a cookout dinner.

We moved to Rattlesnake Cliff near Dillon, Montana, on July 10. Barrett Minerals Inc was located nearby. The company crushed soapstone into talc. Some of our men were able to obtain some soap-stone before it was crushed. The stone was soft and therefore could easily be worked into artistic items. Several of our men made Indian smoking pipes, as described in the journals. We did have a wealth of talent within our ranks.

We put our dugouts back into the water at Rattlesnake Cliff. But before we did, we somehow obtained four aluminum canoes and had some fun on the Beaverhead River. We took the aluminum canoes back upstream to the Clark Canyon Dam and put them in the water below the dam. This gave us a downstream float for about fifteen miles. The river was fairly swift, but not too deep. Alec Weltzien and I were in the third canoe to launch. Things were going fine. Alec was in the bow, and I was in the stern. We came upon a sharp turn in the river and did not have enough speed to negotiate the turn. The river was approximately thirty feet wide. The current carried us into a barbed wire fence that was hanging over a portion of the river. Upon hitting the fence, the canoe turned over. Alec went one way, and I went the other way. Fortunately, Alec fell away from the fence, but unfortunately I fell into the fence. In the scramble, I pretty badly cut my hands on the fence. There were several puncture wounds and a worrisome amount of bleeding. Alec recovered the canoe, emptied the water, and was sitting on the far bank when the next canoe came by. They picked me up and took me to the other side of the river. Alec and I then continued our trip down the river to Rattlesnake Cliff with Alec in the stern. I was more embarrassed than anything else because our canoe was the only one to turn over that morning. But in the afternoon, three out of four of the canoes turned over, so I did not feel too bad after hearing that.

We bandaged my hands and I went into Dillon for a tetanus booster shot. The shot cost $18, but there was a $22 charge to put me into the Montana Health System.

This might be a good time to talk about our health services on the expedition. We were very fortunate to not have had many serious injuries. With a trip this long and so many people involved, it was almost inevitable that someone would be injured. God had really smiled on us.

We did have training in sailing the boats and I am sure that that training prevented some injuries. The men also looked after each other, offering a helping hand when needed. The most serious incident I remember was when one of our men fell off of a gangplank and broke two ribs. Another man ended up in the hospital for a couple of days with pneumonia. There were several injuries by hunting knives, but no hospitalization required.

We also had some minor burns from working around the cooking fires near the kitchen tent.

Blisters on the feet and hands were common. The feet blisters usually occurred when the men would walk miles and miles over the mountain trails. This normally happened when we had more men than horses. These blisters had to be treated to prevent infections

Hand blisters occurred from holding a paddle and rhythmically paddling for hours and hours on end, or swinging an axe to chop or split wood for our kitchen fires, or using period tool like axes, adzes, draw knives, chisels, and two-man handsaws to make dugout canoes. Once again, these blisters had to be treated to prevent infections. Working with wood always brought on the hazards of splinters. The splinters had to be removed and the wound treated to prevent infection.

We were very fortunate to have trained emergency medical technicians (EMT) with us. Dick Brumley was the most prevalent. He probably used the first aid kit more than anyone else because he knew what he was doing.

Pete Murray was a physician's assistant, and when he was on the river, he administered to our medical needs as well. There were several other men who were fire fighters and of course, these guys were also trained for emergencies. Since 83 percent of our members had military experience in their backgrounds, this was a blessing.

In '04 one of our men needed a hospital visit. When the hospital was told that he was with the Discovery Expedition of St. Charles, they tried to bill DESC because the man did not have medical insurance. The following year, it was mandatory that anyone on the river had to have their own medical insurance coverage, or he would not be scheduled for river duty. Medical insurance was something that Captain Lewis did not have to worry about. Things have changed in 200 years.

On July 11, we moved to Twin Bridges, Montana. Twin Bridges was where the Beaverhead River changes names and became bigger. The Ruby River and the Big Hole River join the Beaverhead River at Twin Bridges, and the Beaverhead River then became the Jefferson River. The river was still rather shallow, and we did cordelling while in the area. The local town folks hosted us for a dinner, and we performed our singing for dinner routine with introductions and our signature songs.

Our next encampment was at Lewis and Clark Caverns State Park, Montana, on July 12. The original expedition never saw these caverns because they were not discovered until 1892, many years after the corps passed through the area in 1805 and 1806. The park rangers treated us royally on our return visit. There was a two-hour guided tour of the caverns offered by the park. The tour was over two miles long and downhill after entering the caverns on an upper level of the mountain. Our men were allowed to take the tour, if in uniform, at no cost. Several of the men, who were not with us last year, took advantage of the park's offer.

The Park Rangers assigned us a camping area, which contained a pavilion and was within walking distance of restrooms and showers. The pavilion was covered, enclosed on two sides, and had a concrete floor. There were a dozen or so picnic tables in the pavilion, which could easily seat fifty or sixty people. Within this structure was a built in fireplace for cooking our meals and sinks with running water, quite a setup. That afternoon, the Park Rangers brought a large propane grill, coolers filled with bottled water and soft drinks, and burgers with all the trimmings to our campsite. You guessed it—we had an outstanding meal courtesy of the Park Rangers. But we had to sing for our supper.

As a matter of fact, the rangers had advertised that we would make a presentation on an outdoor stage about a half a mile from our campsite. All park visitors and other interested individuals were invited to attend. After we ate, we walked up to the outdoor theater and started our dog and pony show. It was overcast when we started, and then about fifteen minutes into the show, the lightning began. We immediately abandoned ship and all personnel went to the pavilion in our campsite area. The rain came and we had a deluge for about half an hour. Then things cleared up, a very interesting evening. Even a bad experience is an experience. You may not like it when you are going through it, but it gives you something to talk about when it is over.

On July 13, we returned to Three Forks, Montana. Just like the original expedition, we were now moving rather quickly since we were going downstream and not spending too much time at any one campsite.

Three Forks is where the Jefferson River is joined by the Madison River and the Gallatin River, and they became the Missouri River. We were back on the Missouri River.

Three Forks was also where Captain Clark told Sergeant Ordway to take the dugouts and nine men and continue on down the Missouri River to meet Captain Lewis' men at the Great Falls. We did not have enough men to be historically correct, so all of our men went with our Captain Clark towards the Yellowstone River.

On the original journey, Captain Clark traveled about fifty miles from Three Forks to the Yellowstone River. He arrived at the Yellowstone River somewhere between Livingston, Montana, and Big Timber, Montana, on July 20. Captain Clark had the men build two dugout canoes, and when finished, the dugouts were tied together, catamaran style, and launched onto the Yellowstone River on July 24.

We moved our camp to Livingston, Montana, and spent July 14–15 there. We camped in the Sacagawea Park and were part of a weekend city festival, which included the dedication of a Sacagawea statue.

There were carnival rides and a rock concert that kept us up till an ungodly hour on Friday night. We set up our stations each day and spoke with many interested visitors.

We had been asked to send a contingent of men to Bozeman, Montana, to participate in a presentation being made by the Museum of the Rockies. We gladly complied with their request. The museum had set up displays inside and outside of their building. We set up our displays outside and augmented their presentations, a fun time all day.

We were invited to stay on the Thompson Ranch near Big Timber, Montana, from July 16–19. This was where we launched our dugouts. We had been trailering our four dugout canoes since Three Forks.

Historically, there were only two dugout canoes on the Yellowstone River. But since we did not send Sergeant Ordway down the Missouri River, we brought those dugouts with us because we needed them when we reached the confluence of the Yellowstone River with the Missouri River.

Upon launching all four canoes, two of the canoes were lashed together to make a catamaran. I was impressed with Captain Clark's decision to lash two dugouts together. A dugout canoe was a log, and a log was unstable. I did not like them but when they were lashed together they were very stable and a pleasure to paddle. The only problem was that it was difficult to change sides for paddling when in a catamaran because the other hull was in the way. Changing or switching to the other dugout was the solution. Therefore, it was not unusual for men to change positions when a break was taken. We had an opportunity to get plenty of time on the river while we were at the Thompson Ranch, even though it was not downstream at the time.

The reason we were spending four days at Thompson Ranch was that we were now ahead of the timeline set by the 1806 expedition. Captain Clark arrived at the Yellowstone River on July 20. He then had the men make two dugout canoes, which took four days. He actually launched his canoes on July 24 and arrived at Pompey's Pillar on the famous date of July 25, 1806.

Interesting facts about the 1806 expedition at this time were the horses. Captain Clark had forty-nine horses and twenty-three people with him at Three Forks. When he sent Sergeant Ordway down the Missouri River with nine men, Ordway did not take horses with him because he was waterborne with five or six dugouts. Meanwhile, while Captain Clark's men were making the two dugouts at the Yellowstone River, half of the horses were stolen. When Clark launched his catamaran on July 24, he ordered Sergeant Pryor and three men to take the remaining horses overland to the Mandan Villages. Private Hall was sent on this mission because he could not swim. The next night, all of the horses were stolen. Sergeant

Pryor and his men proceeded to make two bullboats and then set off after Captain Clark. Pryor and his men caught up to Captain Clark on August 8. Bullboats were made by tying willow branches and limbs together for a frame, and then covering the frame with a skin of either buffalo or elk, whichever was available at the time. The boat was perfectly round with no bow or stern, therefore very difficult to steer. The Indians taught the members of the expedition how to make these boats. The journals sometimes referred to these bullboats as leather boats.

We moved camp to Pompey's Pillar National Monument, Montana, on July 20. "Clark on the Yellowstone" was a National Bicentennial Signature Event. Pompey's Pillar is important because that was where Captain Clark carved his name and the date into the sandstone rock. The signature is the only remaining physical evidence that the Corps of Discovery made their fantastic journey 200 years ago. There were numerous comments in the journals that the men left their initials and date on trees, particularly on trees near the shores of the Pacific Ocean. But those trees were long gone. The William Clark July 25, 1806, signature and date were protected from the weather and vandals by a glass enclosure.

We had two camps at Pompey's Pillar. The main camp was a couple of miles from the Pompey's Pillar National Monument site and a smaller camp on the grounds of the historic site. There was so much activity during these five days that there was not enough room at the site for us to set up our full camp.

The feature attraction for this signature event was our Captain Clark cutting William Clark's signature and date into a block of sandstone. This duplicated the event of 200 years ago. During our stay there, we were invited to a beer party at the Yellowstone Valley Brewery in Billings, Montana. Not wanting to offend the beer fairy, we accepted the invitation. The party and heavy hors d'oeuvres were hosted by a sergeant from the Montana National Guard who lived in the area. Naturally, we again sang for our supper. Our performing our signature songs kept the brewery lively for the evening. After all, "Parties Make the World Go Round," and that was the perfect venue for singing that song.

There were several of us who, last year, had missed the Corps' journey through the Missouri Breaks. We now had an opportunity to make that float. The 1803–1806 Corps of Discovery journey was a military expedition and consequently, except for Sacagawea, there were no women on the river. We had a lot of wives and women who were members of our Corps, who supported us and at times traveled with us but never had the opportunity to see the riverbanks from the river. There were also times when we had a family camp near our camp for children and other family members who enjoyed camping out and being part of our adventure. The 2005 journey up the Missouri River through the Missouri Breaks had no women along. Now is the time for the ladies to enjoy the experience of floating down the Missouri River through the Missouri Breaks. Some twenty of us—about half women—traveled to Coal Banks Landing, launched our aluminum canoes, and spent four nights on a river float, exiting at Judith Landing some fifty miles downriver. It was a very memorable float for all of us.

We rejoined the expedition at Glendive, Montana on July 31, then on to Sidney, Montana, and finally arriving at the confluence of the Yellowstone River with the Missouri River on August 7. We revisited Fort Buford's skeletal site, its cemetery, and the fully refurbished Fort Union. The personnel at the Missouri-Yellowstone Confluence Interpretative Center were again very accommodating.

Our next stop was at Trenton Lake State Park, North Dakota, during August 10–13.

One of our members was a graduate of Trenton High School here in Trenton, North Dakota. We visited the local high school and her picture was on the wall as a past graduate. That member was Jan Two Bears Falcon who frequently portrayed Sacagawea for us while we were on the trail.

August 14 finds us in New Town, North Dakota, for the National Bicentennial Signature Event, Reunion at the Home of Sakakawea.

(That is the way her name is spelled locally.) The Mandan, Hidatsa, and Arikara nations put on another outstanding pow-wow. The organizers of this event were commended. It was evident that much time and labor had gone into this event.

We camped on a peninsula a short distance from the Antelope Arbor, which was the center of attraction for this signature event. We set up stations and manned them daily for the many visitors we had at our camp. The six newly constructed earth lodges next to our encampment added a great deal of realism and aesthetic value to the signature event.

The local Indian military veterans invited us to march with them each morning to raise the flag. We gladly accepted the invitation and became a part of the daily routine. Native Americans have a special reverence for military veterans, who were considered warriors. The first dance at every pow-wow is dedicated to honor all veterans. When this dance was started, all veterans in attendance were invited to participate in the dance.

We were also honored to be invited to participate in the daily entrance parades and to be introduced with other honored guests in the arbor.

We again met our friend Jessica Grinnell, who portrayed Sakakawea during the signature event. She helped us last year and blended in with our Corps perfectly.

The contestant dancers with their feathers, bells, sequins, and colorful clothing were again spectacular. The dance competition was awesome.

We were also invited to make presentations in the arbor. These presentations coincided with the theme of the signature event, which was the return of the Corps of Discovery and the returning home of Sakakawea. This was a very enlightening, seven-day encampment.

It was in the Mandan Villages that Sakakawea, her baby, Pomp, and her husband, Charbonneau, left the expedition. It was also here that Private John Colter requested a discharge from the Corps so that he could return to the mountains as a trapper. Captain Lewis said that he could leave if no one else made the same request. No one made such a request, therefore Colter was allowed to leave the Corps at the Mandan Villages.

Even though the Corps lost three people here, it gained several people because Chief Sheheke, with his family, agreed to travel down the river to meet with President Jefferson. When we left the signature event, we had several tribal members on board our white pirogue portraying Chief Shekeke and his family.

New Town, North Dakota was a very impressive stop both times we stopped there during our journey.

We arrived at Fort Mandan on July 21 and were welcomed by David Borlaug and his accommodating staff. We set up our tents and stations in a field next to the overflow parking lot. The use of showers and Internet connections were offered.

The National Guard Bureau had sponsored the 2006 Lewis and Clark Youth Rendezvous, and the North Dakota National Guard hosted the event.

High school students from all over the country were invited to write an essay describing which army value best described the journey of Lewis and Clark and the Corps of Discovery. Approximately 300 students were selected from all fifty states and four territories to participate in the week's activities.

We were an integral part of these activities. The students stayed in military tents at a 4-H campsite and participated in a pontoon boat river movement with a couple of our men on each pontoon boat; this trip ended at a beach party.

The students were also bused to Bismarck, North Dakota's capitol, Fort Lincoln, Fort Mandan, and other points of interest in the area. Their visit to our campsite and cycling through our stations was very well received.

Opening ceremonies for the rendezvous were held at Fort Lincoln State Park, featuring a concert followed by motivational speeches from Presidents Thomas Jefferson, Abraham Lincoln, and Theodor Roosevelt, then Amy Mossett, as Sakakawea, and of course our Captains Meriwether Lewis and William Clark. It was a very interesting few days for the students and for us.

Our next encampment, on July 23, was at Whetstone Bay near Gregory, South Dakota. My grandparents on my father's side are buried in Gregory along with an uncle, his wife, a cousin, and her husband. I stopped at their gravesites to pay my respects.

On our way to Whetstone, four of our men stopped to shoot a buffalo. In 2004, on our trip up the river, we met the owner of a buffalo ranch. We had an interesting conversation with him. He then invited us to shoot one of his buffalo on our return trip. I believe he had a herd of some 800 buffalo and had to cull the herd by 10 percent each year. Consequently, he had to kill about 80 buffalo annually. It took our men four shots from their flintlock rifles to bring the big bull down.

The carcass was brought to our campsite, skinned, and quartered. Since we did not have freezers, we had to take some 400 pounds of buffalo meat to a local processing plant. They packaged and flash froze the meat for us. They also stored the frozen buffalo while we were in the area, a very hospitable gesture. Of course, we had buffalo for the next two weeks at almost every meal.

We were fortunate enough to have the good people of South Dakota help us with moving our frozen buffalo meat from storage area to storage area as we traveled down the Missouri River. Before we quartered the buffalo, we were hosted to a catered cookout by members of the local Lewis and Clark Bicentennial Committee. We were again grateful to many friendly souls for their generosity and hospitality.

We moved on and arrived at Yankton, South Dakota, on July 24. Gavin's Point Dam is located at Yankton. There was no lock at this dam. Consequently, we had to portage around the dam. The highlight about this portage was that it was the last portage on the Missouri River. We had now traversed all six dams on the upper Missouri. All we needed to do now was find a deep enough channel in the river to arrive in St. Louis over 800 miles downstream. While camped in Yankton, Bob Anderson and I traveled to Niobrara, Nebraska, to participate in a parade. We were part of a Lewis and Clark float bearing a replica of the keelboat. We had a great time with the local town folks.

On July 29, we were in Burbank, South Dakota, and camped in the backyard of Pete Murray's home. Pete was one of our crewmembers and a physician's assistant. He attended to our medical needs when he was on the river. It is nice to have friends with big backyards.

His property was on the Missouri River and had a boat dock, but his dock was not large enough to accommodate our pirogue. His neighbor was nice enough to allow us to tie the pirogue up to his dock. Once again, it was a hospitable gesture by one of our fellow Americans. Naturally, the neighbor received one of our crew medals. Our four dugouts were okay at Pete's dock.

Pete was a drummer in a local rock and roll band. He brought his band members together to give us a rock concert in his backyard. What can I say? Where else, except on the Lewis and Clark reenactment could you find this type of homespun entertainment? We had to knock the music off at eleven o'clock because of the neighbors. But that was okay because the beer fairy had visited camp, so all was well.

From September 1–3, we camped at Ponca, Nebraska, and then on to Sioux City, Iowa, for September 3–4. Here we met with the Sergeant Floyd Brigade again and had a memorial ceremony at Floyd's Monument. We fired a salute to Sergeant Floyd. When the 1806 corps stopped here on September 4, they found Floyd's grave had been partially opened. The men filled and covered the grave completely before continuing their journey downriver.

Then on to Decatur, Nebraska, for September 5. On our way to Decatur, we paddled to a landing on the Omaha Indian Reservation. We were met by several members of the Omaha Tribe who welcomed us onto their reservation. They gifted us with several items. Each member of our corps received a t-shirt that said "Rezhunter" with an Indian warrior on it. They also gave us an Omaha tribal flag. We responded with our crew medals and an American fifteen stars and fifteen stripes flag.

Once again, we were able to reach out to our Native American brothers and sisters to try to forge a healing process that was so richly deserved.

Then on to Wilson Island State Park, Iowa, for September 6. The next day we arrived in Omaha, Nebraska. Upon arrival in Omaha, we tied our dugouts up in a new sheltered municipal marina. Walked to the United States Army Corps of Engineers Omaha District Headquarters and were welcomed by a member of the staff. Then we were given a tour of the ground floor of the building, and were told that if we needed anything, just ask. We told them that we needed lunch. We were escorted to a local waterfront restaurant and had lunch.

The next day, September 8, we moved on to Plattsmouth, Nebraska, where we were hosted to meals at Mike Bowman's home. Mike is a member of our crew and one of the members of the famous Mike and Ed boat.

He and his wife, Joyce, did an outstanding job of preventing us from starving. The meal they served at their home was much appreciated. The good folks of Plattsmouth had planned a parade for our benefit. We marched in their parade to the cheers of the crowds lining the streets, another example of the hospitality we were experiencing all along the Lewis and Clark trail. We were in Plattsmouth for two nights.

As you can see we were moving quickly down the river, just as the 1806 expedition did. They were doing sixty, seventy, or more miles per day at that time. Our next stop, on September 10, was Nebraska City, Nebraska; we then moved on to Rulo, Nebraska, on September 11. We spent September 12–13 in Atchison, Kansas, and September 14 in Fort Leavenworth, Kansas. The 1806 expedition set the timeline for us. In many of our stops, we were welcomed by mayors and other dignitaries with ceremonies covered by the local press and television. The 1806 expedition did not have to worry about such commitments. In order to meet these commitments and to be on time for a scheduled arrival, the dugouts were towed by the pirogue rather than being trailered to the event.

Kaw Point was our next destination for 15–16 of September. Kaw

Point was at the confluence of the Kansas River with the Missouri River and had a beautiful view of the Kansas City skyline. The waterfront park at this location was one of the best we had visited. Our campsite was very convenient to the boats and has plenty of room.

You may recall that this is where Privates John Collins and Hugh Hall were court-martialed for drinking Corps whiskey in June, 1804. As a point of interest there were seven court-martials on the trip involving twelve men. The first was on March 29, 1804, when Privates John Shields, John Colter, and Robert Frazer were charged with misconduct. Then May 17, 1804, when Privates William Warner and Hugh Hall were charged with absence without leave and John Collins was charged with absence without leave, bad conduct at the ball, and speaking disrespectfully to the Captain. On June 29, 1804, Privates Hugh Hall and John Collins were charged with drinking Corps whiskey; on July 12, 1804, Private Alexander Willard was charged with sleeping on sentry duty; on August 18, 1804, Private Moses Reed was charged with desertion; and then October 13, 1804, Private John Newman was charged with making mutinous expressions. Lastly, on February 10, 1805, Private Thomas Howard was charged with entering the fort by climbing over the wall after dark. All court-martials resulted in convictions with various punishments being given to the offenders ranging from banishment from the corps to commuted sentences.

A half a dozen of our men should have been court-martialed: first, Hebe, for outrageous conduct; Ed Falvo, for hiding of food; Derek Biddle, for unauthorized swimming; Concrete, for making a horse sway back; Walter Gotsch for wearing smoked leather clothing and finally, Bryant Boswell, for failure to lower the flag at 1700 hours. I am not going to elaborate on these charges, but the next time you speak with one of our crewmembers, ask him about the conduct of these men. I am sure that they will fill you in on the details and will probably add a name or two to this infamous list of men who should have been court-martialed.

We spent September 17 and 18 at Lupus, Missouri, whose population was twenty-nine. There were forty of us on the river at that time. Consequently, we more than doubled the town's population, but the good folks of Lupus took care of us like long lost friends. They fed us and had a golden throne (toilet) installed for us since our last visit in 2004. The Order of the Pink Flamingo was given to Josh Loftis. In 2004, the honor went to Bob Anderson, or was it the other way around? Anyway, Lupus opened their hearts to us. It was stops like this that brought out the true spirit of our American camaraderie. It made me so proud to be an American.

On September 19, we were welcomed to Jefferson City, Missouri, by Mayor John Landwehr. We were permitted to camp in a beautiful park and fed substantial meals, which included ice cream. When we started getting ice cream at dinner, we thought that we must be getting near the journey's end.

The next day, September 20, we travel to Washington, Missouri, and were again greeted by the friends we had made in 2004 on our journey up the Missouri River. Every stop was now like a reunion because we had been there before and were being welcomed back with open arms. Unfortunately, we were missing a lot of stops because we are traveling great distances on the river each day. On the way up the river, we were fighting currents and some times made only eight miles in a day. Now that we are going down the river, we were doing up to eighty miles in a day.

We arrived at St. Charles, Missouri, on September 21, and we were welcomed by a tumultuous crowd of well-wishers. I believe that the entire population of St .Charles and then some were on the bank to help us tie up. It was a joyous homecoming. We were not quite finished, but for the people of St. Charles we were home. The next day, we traveled to Fort Bellefontaine, Missouri, for a landing and another welcoming. The 1806 expedition camped at Fort Bellfontaine the night before they arrived at St. Louis. So to be historically correct, we made an appearance at Fort Bellefontaine on September 22.

September 23 was the end of this epic journey at St. Louis. We had eighty-three men in uniform, the largest number of our men in one place at any one time during the entire three-year journey. We could put only thirty or so men on the boats, but the rest of us were in the welcoming party as the boats pulled in.

There must have been six thousand people on the river bank to welcome us back. We all lined up in front of a new Lewis and Clark statue, and dignitaries made welcoming speeches and presentations to key people. Chief Sheheke and his family were commended for their traveling to St. Louis. It was a very festive occasion.

My brother and sister-in-law, a nephew, a niece and their two children were also there to welcome me home. They all came from Philadelphia. Being welcomed back by your family has a special meaning.

The conclusion of our journey had mixed emotions for me. It would be nice to start sleeping in a bed again. But the camaraderie of the men on the trail was missing. Looking back the thing I missed most were the nightly campfires. These cannot be duplicated anywhere except on the trail. There was something magical about men sitting around a campfire in the woods, on a mountain or on a river bank and singing and talking.

You got to know your fellow crew members by their walk or their silhouette or their posture or the clothing they wore. You could recognize a man at a distance through these attributes.

I am sure that the men on the original expedition had mixed emotions also but most of all were happy to be back safely. I have no doubt that they bonded with their fellow crew members just as we have bonded and made life long friends.

All of our crewmembers felt a sense of accomplishment, and well we should because if you look back at what we accomplished, we are a close second to the original expedition. No other organization in our American history has ever completed such a long and laborious reenactment. The Discovery Expedition of St. Charles has established a benchmark that I do not see being broken in the near future or the far future. Glen Bishop is certainly smiling.

Epilogue

In the spring of 2005, I was on guard duty at Fort Mandan, North Dakota, and had a conversation with Pennsylvania State Representative Lynn Herman, who was the representative for the 77th Pennsylvania Legislative District. When he learned that I was a Pennsylvania resident, we went into great detail about my involvement with this commemorative reenactment of the Lewis and Clark Expedition. During our discussion, he stated that he was a Civil War reenactor for a Pennsylvania unit. At the conclusion of our discussion, he stated that he would look into the possibility of recognition for my portrayal of Private Hugh Hall, a fellow Pennsylvanian, during our three-year reenactment.

As a result of Representative Herman's efforts, on June 6, 2006, I was presented to the Pennsylvania House of Representatives in full period dress uniform and honored with the following resolution:

A Resolution

Commending Edwin Scholl for his four-year portrayal of Private Hugh Hall as a member of the Discovery Expedition of Saint Charles, Missouri during the bicentennial commemoration of the Lewis and Clark Expedition.

Whereas, Edwin Scholl, of North Wales, Pennsylvania was a member of the reenactment group following the original Lewis and Clark Expedition, which reenactment spans the years 2003 through 2006; and

Whereas, the reenactors, known as the Discovery Expedition of Saint Charles, Missouri, retraced the movements of the original Lewis and Clark Expedition through the area of the United States annexed by the Louisiana Purchase of 1803; and

Whereas, through the Discovery Expedition of Saint Charles, Missouri, Mr. Scholl portrayed fellow Pennsylvanian Private Hugh Hall of Carlisle, Pennsylvania, who was a member of the original Lewis and Clark Expedition; and

Whereas, Mr. Scholl began his role in Elizabeth, Pennsylvania, where many feel the keelboat was built, and traveled twenty-two miles down the Monongahela River, 973 miles down the Ohio River, and 192 miles up the Mississippi River to the winter encampment of 1803 at Camp Dubois, Illinois; and

Whereas, in the spring of 2004, the reenactors then traveled 1500 miles up the Missouri River to the winter encampment of 1804 at Fort Mandan, North Dakota; and

Whereas, from Fort Mandan, North Dakota the reenactors followed the Missouri River to its headwaters, then crossed the Bitterroot Mountains on horseback to Canoe Camp near Orofino, Idaho where they built dugout canoes and paddled the canoes down the Clearwater River, to the Snake River, to the Columbia River, and finally to the Pacific Ocean and Fort Clatsop, Oregon; and

Whereas, the reenactors followed the Lewis and Clark journals by camping at the locations indicated in the journals and viewing the geographical features noted in the journals in an effort to be as realistic as possible and living the true Lewis and Clark experience; and

Whereas, the reenactment drew large crowds during their 8,000-mile journey and imparted unique Lewis and Clark educational information to thousands of schoolchildren and other interested visitors who arrived at their camps; and

Whereas, Mr. Scholl gave up significant portions of his time and considerable costs for uniforms and accouterments to recreate this famous expedition; therefore be it

Resolved, that the House of Representatives commend Edwin Scholl for portraying Private Hugh Hall and for participating in the 2003–2006 reenactment of the historic Lewis and Clark Expedition throughout the upper portions of the Louisiana Purchase; and be it further

Resolved, that a copy of this resolution be transmitted to Edwin Scholl, 204 Highland Court, North Wales, Pennsylvania, 19454.

Photos

Discovery Expedition of St Charles Gift Medals

Keelboat

Keelboat Trailered for Portaging

Red Pirogue

White Pirogue

Boats Tented for Sleeping

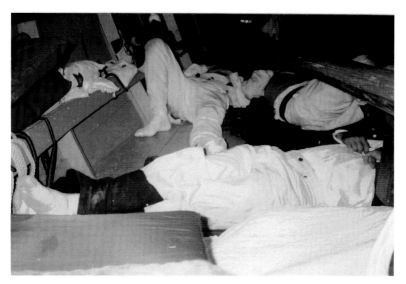

Sleeping in Tented Boats

Dugout Canoe

Making Dugout Canoes at Canoe Camp

Our Chinook Canoe—Its WOOT—at Netul Landing

Catamaran on the Yellowstone River

Sodding the Roofs at Camp Dubois

Erecting Palisades at Camp Dubois

Seaman at Camp Dubois

Assemblying Inside Camp Dubois

Prayer Prior to Departure Up the Missouri River

Morning on the Missouri River

Aerial View of Boats Docked at Atchison, KS July 4th

School Students at Fort Mandan Showing Us the Way

Canoes Going Under Fire Hose Welcome at Ulm, MT

Going Through Gates of the Rocky Mountains with Interested Spectators

Lunch on the Missouri River

Idaho Side of Lemhi Pass

A Valley in Idaho

Lowering Flag at Lost Trail Hot Springs Camp

Rapids on the Clearwater River

Our First Sunset on the Pacific Ocean

Jessica Grinnell as Sacagawea and the Author

Indian Pow-Wow at Newtown, North Dakota

End of our Journey in St Louis

Welcoming Ceremony in St Louis

The Honorable Lynn Herman and the Author in the
Pennsylvania House of Representatives Chambers